PAUL
and His Predecessors

PAUL
and His Predecessors

ARCHIBALD M. HUNTER

Philadelphia
THE WESTMINSTER PRESS

Contents

Abbreviations

EGT	*Expositor's Greek Testament*
ET	English translation
Ex.T	*Expository Times*
HNT	*Handbuch zum Neuen Testament*
ICC	International Critical Commentary
JBL	*Journal of Biblical Literature*
JTS	*Journal of Theological Studies*
Meyer	*Kritisch-exegetisches Kommentar über das Neue Testament,* begründet von H. A. W. Meyer
MNTC	Moffatt New Testament Commentary
SJT	*Scottish Journal of Theology*
Str. Bill.	H. L. Strack and P. Billerbeck, *Kommentar zum Neuen Testament aus Talmud und Midrasch,* I–IV, 1922–8
Th.Wb.	*Theologisches Wörterbuch zum Neuen Testament,* ed. G. Kittel, 1933 ff.
WC	Westminster Commentary
ZNTW	*Zeitschrift für die neutestamentliche Wissenschaft*

I · The Problem

WE HAVE, IN THE PAST, EXAGGERATED ST PAUL'S ORIGINALITY and creativeness. He was to an extent we have never fully realized indebted to the Christianity which existed before and alongside of him. There is much in St Paul's theology and thinking that is common and apostolic.

Let it be granted that Paul's is a highly original and seminal mind; that on occasion (as in Gal. 1.11 ff. written, however, with his nerves in 'a kind of blaze') he defiantly protests his spiritual independence of his apostolic predecessors; that his own idiosyncrasy counted for much in his presentation of the Gospel. Nevertheless, to suppose that Paul's Christianity is simply the working-out of things theological and ethical in the light of one forever memorable experience on the road to Damascus, or that he derived most of what we call Paulinism from special revelations, or that he was an arch-innovator in such matters as the conception of Christ's person or the doctrine of his piacular death or the view of the Lord's Supper expressed in I Cor. 11—all such suppositions seem to me unsound. Paul depended in many ways on pre-Pauline Christianity. 'Early Christianity was an epic, but just as there were other heroes than Hector or Achilles before the walls of Ilium, and other *revénants* than Odysseus so there were other heroes of the apostolic age than St Paul.'[1]

Our task is to discover something of that dependence. Here let me anticipate a certain criticism. I am aware that the term 'pre-Pauline', if it suggests the period of early Christian history (not more than five years) between the crucifixion and Paul's conversion, is misleading. I use the term for lack of a better. By it I mean 'the twilight period' between the rise of the Christian church and the decade in which Paul's extant letters were written.

[1] Weiss, *History of Primitive Christianity*, I, p. ix. (Translator's Preface.)

It is not proposed to treat exhaustively the whole field of Pauline religion and ethics—to write yet another treatise on Pauline theology. My aim is to prove that Paul owed much to his precursors 'in Christ'. I cannot hope to lay bare all Paul's dependence on the pre-Pauline Christian tradition. My intention is to choose certain clearly-marked evidences of Paul's dependence on pre-Pauline Christianity, and to investigate these in turn. If I can do this successfully, I shall have accomplished the better part of my purpose, which is to take Paul out of his apostolic insularity and to set him in the midst of early Christianity—to see him not as a lone pioneer blazing, single-handed, the trail of early Christianity, but as one of a gallant company of pioneers; or (to change the figure) to see him not as a sort of spiritual Columbus 'voyaging through strange seas of thought alone', but as one sailing (as the historical Paul did sail) in company with others in the apostolic ship. To do this service for Paul is absolutely necessary, if we are to understand the man and his achievement aright. And to do it is not to rob Paul of his nimbus, but to see this dynamic and creative apostle of Christ against the background of primitive and apostolic Christianity.

This is not the old problem: how much did Paul know of the Jesus of history? Yet the two problems overlap; for while some of Paul's knowledge of the historic Jesus must have been garnered in his pre-Christian days, much also must have come to him from the tradition current in the Church when he was converted.

Let us clear the way to the major problem by first giving a brief answer to the question: How much did Paul know of the historic Jesus? I waive the question whether Paul ever saw Jesus in the flesh. That is a question on which (*pace* J. Weiss and others) we can only return the Scottish verdict of Not Proven.

What can we glean from the epistles concerning Paul's knowledge of the Jesus of history?

Jesus was a man (Rom. 5.15; I Cor. 15.21); and a Jew (Rom. 9.5); born of a woman and under the Law (Gal. 4.4); a descendant of Abraham (Gal. 3.16); and of David's line (Rom. 1.3). He had brothers (I Cor. 9.5) one of whom was called James (Gal. 1.19). He carried on a ministry among the Jews (Rom. 15.8).

If Paul seems strangely silent about the Galilean ministry, he knows that Jesus had a disciple-band (I Cor. 15.5) twelve in number. Moreover, certain casual phrases in the epistles hint that he had a warm appreciation of the character of the historic Jesus. His reference to 'the meekness and gentleness of Christ' (II Cor. 10.1) recalls the self-description of Jesus as the 'meek and lowly in heart' (Matt. 11.29). Elsewhere Paul speaks of his 'obedience' (Rom. 5.19), 'endurance' (II Thess. 3.5), and his 'grace' (II Cor. 8.9). No doubt, in II Cor. 8.9, Paul is thinking primarily of the divine condescension involved in the Incarnation—the Christmas paradox, as the Germans call it—but his choice of the verb ἐπτώχευσεν would have been inept if he had not known that the earthly lot of Jesus was not one of affluence. Many consider I Cor. 13.4–7 Paul's pen-portrait of Christ. More significant are his words in I Cor. 11.1, 'Be ye imitators of me, even as I also am of Christ', when read in the light of Weiss's comment. 'It is a very important trait, that Paul feels himself to be an imitator of Christ in his practical conduct. He could not say and be this, unless he had a living, concrete picture of the ethical personality of Jesus.'[1]

Of the closing scenes in the earthly life of Jesus Paul shows more knowledge. He knows that Jesus was 'delivered up' and that it was on that night that he instituted the Lord's Supper (I Cor. 11.23–5). In I Cor. 5.7 where he speaks of Christ as the Christians' paschal lamb he possibly betrays a knowledge of the exact date of the crucifixion. The Jews compassed his death (I Thess. 2.15). The mode of it was crucifixion (I Cor. 2.8; Gal. 3.13). He was buried, raised on the third day, and appeared to many witnesses (I Cor. 15.3 ff.).

Paul also knew something of Christ's teaching. Four times in the epistles he alludes to 'Words of the Lord' (I Cor. 7.10, 9.14, 11.23–5; I Thess. 4.15–17). These four passages do not exhaust his knowledge of what Jesus had said. Other sayings of Jesus are sometimes inserted tacitly in the hortatory sections of his epistles. Suffice it now to say that I Thess. 5 and Rom. 12 warrant the conclusion that 'Paul had not only yielded to the inspiration of Jesus, but had given careful study to the tradition of his teaching and based his own ethic on a profound understanding of it.'[2]

To many this sum-total of Paul's knowledge of the historic Jesus may seem disappointingly meagre. But for this meagreness there are

---

[1] Weiss, *I Kor.*, p. 267.   [2] Dodd, *Romans*, p. 208.

good reasons. First, it is true to say that Paul's gaze was chiefly fixed not on the Jesus of history but on the risen and regnant Lord. Second, the character of the epistles is *didaché*, not *kerygma*. In the epistles Paul is not setting forth the cardinal facts of the gospel story for those who had never heard of Jesus: he is writing occasional letters to meet the practical needs of Christian communities to whom the fundamentals of the *kerygma* had been already proclaimed. If now and then we do light on allusions to the gospel story, it is because circumstances compel him to disclose his knowledge. One example for many: 'Had it not been for some irreverent behaviour at Corinth, we might never have known what Paul believed about the Lord's Supper.'[1] Just such a passage as this strongly suggests that Paul knew much more about the message and mission of the historic Jesus than he has revealed in his letters.

Even Paul the persecutor must have known the chief facts about the founder of the new sect of the Nazarenes. His fellow Pharisees in Jerusalem certainly did. If Paul was in Jerusalem before and after the crucifixion he must have heard from them 'the things concerning Jesus of Nazareth'. Lacking such knowledge (however caricatured the version) he could not have been a successful persecutor.

Again, Paul was received into the Christian church in the same way as any other convert. The catechists in Damascus must have 'filled up what was lacking' in his knowledge of the tenets of the new faith.

Moreover, after his conversion Paul had many chances to increase his knowledge of what Jesus had said, done, and been. 'Paul did not live in a vacuum. He lived in the primitive Christian society in which all that was known of Jesus was current.'[2] Did he learn nothing about Jesus during his fortnight's stay in Jerusalem when he went up expressly to 'interview' Peter? 'We may presume', comments C. H. Dodd drily, 'that they did not spend all their time talking about the weather.'[3] Then also he met 'James, the Lord's brother'—surely a significant meeting. Besides all this, Paul was a fellow-missionary of many who had been members of the Jerusalem mother-church—Barnabas, Mark, Silas, Jesus Justus (I tumble out the names almost at random), and others. Nor have we yet mentioned 'the beloved

[1] Moffatt, *Grace in the New Testament*, p. 157.
[2] Denney, *Jesus and the Gospel*, p. 21. [3] *Apostolic Preaching*, p. 26.

physician' (the author, as I believe, of Luke–Acts). In brief, we may be tolerably sure that Paul did not stop his ears against what these men had to tell about the life and teaching of their common Lord. The assertion, so often lightly made in discussion, that Paul knew next to nothing about the historic Jesus, is utterly improbable.

This problem behind us, we are now ready to face the major question—What is Paul's debt to the Christianity which existed before and alongside of him? How much of the common apostolic Christianity current, say, between AD 30 and 50 can we detect with some certainty in Paul's epistles?

I have already tried to define the term 'pre-Pauline'. The word 'tradition' I employ in a wide sense. It denotes not merely the specifically doctrinal elements (as in I Cor. 15.3 ff.) but *kerygma*, sacraments, 'Words of the Lord', hymns, and so on—even Paul's use of the Old Testament.

What are the sources? Pre-eminently, the epistles themselves. All, except the Pastorals, are accepted.

The second source is Acts. Although few can go all the way with Torrey, most scholars nowadays admit not only that Luke used earlier sources in compiling Acts 1–15 but that some of these sources were originally in Aramaic. It is usual to discover three distinct sources (*a*) a Jerusalem source, (*b*) a Caesarean source, (*c*) an Antiochian source; but all attempts to get back to these sources are more or less conjectural. The safest conclusion is that 'First Acts' is based on distinct collections of narratives connected with Jerusalem and Antioch, that Aramaic originals glimmer through certain portions (notably 1.1–5.16 and 9.31–11.18), and that therefore we are dealing with primitive materials. More particularly, it is probable that the speeches of Peter, if they do not preserve his *ipsissima verba*, reflect early Jerusalem *kerygma*. They contain numerous Aramaisms (especially e.g. Acts 10.34–43), and their Christology is probably pre-Pauline.

If the Apostolic Fathers cannot be called a third source, they occasionally afford help, just as do the later books of the New Testament.

One more observation. In research of this kind the Epistle to the Romans is specially valuable. Paul did not found the church in Rome, nor had he, when he wrote Romans, ever visited it. Other men, on whose names oblivion has fallen, laid the foundations of that church. Thus we may surmise that wherever in the Epistle to the Romans Paul appeals confidently to *data* of the Christian faith he alludes to something that the leaders of the Roman Church held in common with himself. Elements of the Christian message or scraps of *kerygma* introduced into this epistle as though they were widely current, familiar, almost axiomatic, we may surely reckon as part not only of what Paul styles 'my gospel', but also of the common apostolic gospel—in short, finger-posts pointing back to the pre-Pauline Christianity we are seeking.

We are ready now to start on our quest. Altogether, it is 'a little-trodden, difficult, and dangerous way'—this road into the twilight regions of pre-Pauline Christianity.

II · Pre-Pauline Paradosis

1. LET ME BEGIN WITH A PIECE OF WIDELY ACKNOWLEDGED
pre-Pauline *paradosis* or tradition (I Cor. 15.3 ff.).

> For I delivered (παρέδωκα) unto you first of all that which I also
> received (παρέλαβον), how that (ὅτι) Christ died for (ὑπέρ) our sins
> according to the scriptures; and that (ὅτι) he was buried; and that (ὅτι)
> he hath been raised on the third day according to the scriptures; and
> that (ὅτι, for the fourth time) he appeared to Cephas; then to the
> Twelve; then he appeared to above five hundred brethren at once[1] (of
> whom the greater part remain until now, but some are fallen asleep);
> then he appeared to James; then to all the apostles; and last of all, as
> unto one born out of due time, he appeared unto me (RV).

Of all the survivals of pre-Pauline Christianity in the Pauline
corpus this is unquestionably the most precious. It is our pearl of
great price. We may well be grateful to the Corinthians for their
doubts about the resurrection; otherwise, Paul might never have
been prompted to give us this priceless fragment of *paradosis*. That
it is *paradosis* several facts unite to show:

The verbs Paul uses here are equivalent to the official Jewish
terms for the transmission and the reception of tradition.[2]

ὅτι, 'that', given four times, is tantamount to quotation marks,
and suggests a formula.

Verse 11 of this chapter expressly declares that what has just been
recounted (perhaps 'recited' is the better word) is no private *credo*
of the writer but the *kerygma* of all the apostles, of Peter and James
no less than Paul—'Whether then it be I or they, *so* we preached
and so ye believed.'

An incidental proof: in this chapter Paul's argument deals only

---

[1] Or 'once for all'.   [2] Dibelius, *From Tradition to Gospel*, p. 21.

15

with the resurrection. Why does he drag in the *death* and *burial* of Jesus—items not strictly relevant to the argument—unless it be that they formed part of the formula he is recalling?

We are justified in regarding this passage as a piece of pre-Pauline *paradosis*. I say, 'a piece', for probably it is only a fragment of a larger whole.

The first question is—What are the limits of the formula?

Two things are certain. (1) The final clause—'And last of all, as unto one born out of due time, he appeared to me also'—is Paul's personal testimony, not a part of the formula. (2) 'Of whom the greater part remain until now, but some are fallen asleep' is a parenthesis inserted by Paul to underline the good attestation of this appearance. 'Most of these five hundred', he advises the Corinthian sceptics, 'are still living. If you doubt my word, ask them.'

But is all that remains—formula? Five clauses certainly stood in the original formula:

Christ died for our sins according to the scriptures
He was buried
He hath been raised on the third day according to the scriptures
He appeared to Cephas
Then to the Twelve.

It is not certain that the remaining appearances (viz. 'to above five hundred brethren', 'to James', and 'to all the apostles') belong to the formula. Possibly, since they are not embraced by the ὅτι of quotation, they did not. Their exclusion, however, would not matter much for our purpose; for the crucial statements stand in the first five clauses.

Where did Paul receive this piece of formulated tradition, and when? Did he receive it when he was first admitted into the Christian church? Or when he became a missionary? Or during his fortnight's stay in Jerusalem?

We do not certainly know. The usual theory is that this passage is part of what Paul learned when he went up to Jerusalem to 'learn Peter's story'. The form of the passage—it sounds so obviously a bit of catechism—does not suggest something learned in conversation. Much more likely is the view that Paul is here reproducing the baptismal creed of the Damascus church—a creed perhaps taught to him by Ananias before his baptism. This formula, or something like it, must have formed part of the 'catechesis' which Theophilus and other Christians received upon conversion (Luke 1.1–4).

At all events, our passage must date back to the first decade after the crucifixion, and rightly does Meyer pronounce it 'the oldest document of the Christian church we possess'.[1]

Does this formula represent Palestinian or Hellenistic tradition?

Heitmüller[2] (and after him Bousset) maintained that it was a sort of evangelic summary current in the Hellenistic Christianity of Antioch, Damascus, and Tarsus, and argued that such a summary differed radically from that current in Palestinian circles. Now it is probable, as I have already suggested, that Paul did receive this tradition in a Hellenistic *milieu*; but I can find no cogent evidence for the thesis that there were two quite distinct and different Christian traditions, as Heitmüller declares.

May we not trust Paul when he expressly tells us that the version of the gospel which he delivered to the Corinthians was the same as that preached by the apostles? And although conclusive proof of the ultimate origin of this tradition is impossible, what clues the passage itself affords—the mention of 'The Twelve', the use of the Aramaic 'Cephas', the double emphasis on the Old Testament scriptures, the fact that the witnesses of the risen Jesus are Jerusalemites—seem to point back to Palestinian Christianity.

Nor again (to carry the exchanges into Bousset's own camp) do I think this is quite the kind of gospel summary likely to have been drawn up by Hellenists who had transmogrified Christianity into a full-blown mystery cult—a cult for which the Christ of traditional dogma became 'a generalized blend of Attis, Osiris, and Mithras, wearing as a not too-well-fitting mask the features of Jesus of Nazareth'.[3]

We conclude that wherever Paul received this tradition, it emanated originally from the primitive Palestinian church.

Historically, the passage is of capital importance. It is our earliest evidence for the resurrection of Jesus, dating from a time when eyewitnesses of the events, which it authenticates, could still be found. But on this point, important though it is, I do not dwell now.

Take the passage as a whole. It gives us a fair idea of the content

[1] *Anfänge*, p. 210.   [2] *ZNTW*, XIII, 1912, pp. 320–37.
[3] N. P. Williams, *Essays Catholic and Critical*, p. 391.

of the early gospel. The apostolic *kerygma* centred in the death and resurrection of Jesus, interpreted as the fulfilment of Old Testament prophecy. Notice that there is no reference to the Galilean ministry of Jesus. Are we to conclude that the earliest preachers (unlike their modern counterparts) made no allusion to it? If this passage is a complete whole, we might infer that they made none. But, if as seems likely, it is only a fragment, then there was surely a reference to the time when Jesus 'went about doing good and healing all that were oppressed with the devil' (Acts 10.38). At any rate it is tolerably certain that the early preachers did tell their audiences something of the pre-crucifixion events in the life of Jesus.[1]

Two points in our passage call for special comment. First, the clause, 'how that Christ died for our sins'. This is part of what Paul 'received', and it decisively refutes all who attribute the creation of the doctrine of Christ's piacular death to Paul. Such a doctrine, however rudimentary, existed very early in the Christian church. This fact is very important for the ensuing investigation.

Second, the twice-repeated 'according to the scriptures'. Both the death and resurrection of Jesus are described as the fulfilment of Old Testament prophecy. The precise scriptures are not indicated. What matters is the proof that the Christians from the earliest days made the fulfilment of the Old Testament scriptures in the gospel facts a cardinal part of their message[2] (cf. Rom. 1.2, and the early speeches in Acts).

The early Christian message was set in a framework of 'realized eschatology'. The fulfilment of prophecy means that the Day of the Lord of which the Old Testament prophets had dreamed and prophesied is now become an actuality. In the life, death, and resurrection of Jesus, and in the outpouring of the Spirit, the new era has dawned and Christians are already 'tasting the powers of the age to come' (Heb. 6.5; cf. Barn. i.7).

2. The second piece of *paradosis* preserved in St Paul's letters is the narrative of the Lord's Supper (I Cor. 11.23–25).

> For I received of the Lord that which also I delivered unto you, how that the Lord Jesus in the night in which he was betrayed took bread;

---

[1] See Weiss, *The History of Primitive Christianity*, pp. 225-7.
[2] If particular passages are in view, they probably are Isaiah 53 (for the Death) and Hosea 6. 2. (for the Resurrection). Cf. my *Work and Words of Jesus*, p. 107.

and when he had given thanks he brake it, and said, This is my body which is for you: this do in remembrance of me. In like manner also the cup, after supper, saying, this cup is the new covenant in my blood: this do, as oft as ye drink it, in remembrance of me (RV).

This passage raises many problems:

What does 'I received of the Lord' signify?

What is the literary character of this narrative?

Where did Paul get it?

How does it stand to our other primary account of the Last Supper in Mark 14?

What are we to say of the words, 'This do in remembrance of me', which occur only in the Pauline account of the Last Supper?

Let us take them in turn.

'I received of the Lord' (παρέλαβον ἀπὸ τοῦ κυρίου) does *not* mean that what Paul proceeds to quote came to him through a special private revelation.

1. Paul uses here the same technical terms for 'receiving' and 'transmitting' an oral tradition as he does in I Cor. 15.3 ff. It is natural to understand these terms in the same sense here as there.

2. The form of the passage tells against such a view. It is a 'pericope' full of un-Pauline words. (We shall have more to say on this point presently.)

3. If a special direct revelation had been in Paul's mind, he would have used the preposition παρά, not ἀπό. Four times elsewhere (Gal. 1.12; I Thess. 2.13, 4.1; II Thess. 3.6) he employs παραλαμβάνειν with a preposition. In each case it is παρά and signifies direct receipt; ἀπό here indicates the *ultimate* source.

4. Nowhere else when settling practical problems in his churches does Paul invoke the authority of a special revelation.

5. This account is too like that in the synoptic tradition to warrant the belief that it is the substance of a special revelation.

6. 'From the Lord' is simply another way of saying what he said a few chapters before, 'Not I, but the Lord' (I Cor. 7.10). Paul emphasizes that the ultimate authority for what he quotes is the Lord himself. When Paul says concerning the marriage question, 'Not I, but the Lord,' it is never suggested that he is thinking of a special revelation made to him by the exalted Jesus. Nor should we draw that inference here.

I Cor. 11.23–25 is, therefore, like I Cor. 15.3 ff., a piece of *paradosis* mediated to Paul by the pre-Pauline church.

What is the literary character of the narrative? First, a word on the style and vocabulary. The style is elevated, almost rhetorical, with parallelism running through it and a refrain-like ending. When we examine the diction, we find that δειπνέω, ὁσάκις and ἀνάμνησις occur only here in Paul. Nor can we parallel the neat μετὰ τὸ δειπνῆσαι in the Pauline corpus. Now, the form-critics have pointed out that this passage is an excellent example of those isolated narratives once current orally in the church which went to the making of the synoptic tradition. If this be so, we have to ask, What was its 'setting in life'—its essential character? It is an aetiological cult-narrative. By this we mean not a story freely invented to justify an existing rule but a story influenced by the practice of worship. 'What he (Paul) records', says Otto,[1] 'is clearly traditional material long since rounded off, a piece of tradition which had long possessed a firm ritual and which he simply had received, as he himself says.' In short, this was the liturgical form of words used in administering the Lord's Supper in some pre-Pauline church.

But which church? Whence and when did Paul derive this narrative?

Probably he first heard the words in Damascus after his conversion. It was in Damascus that the converted Paul was received into the Christian community. Since he received baptism there, it is altogether likely that there too he first came to know the sacramental table-fellowship of the Christian church. If this be so, this bit of tradition must rank with I Cor. 15.3 ff. in antiquity. Moreover, the tradition which the narrative enshrines, with its careful notes of time ('the night in which he was delivered up', 'after supper'), must have come originally from the primitive church in Jerusalem, must go back ultimately to those who were present on the occasion of the Last Supper.

How does the narrative stand to the other primary account of the Last Supper in Mark 14? Which has the more claim to be original? This is a hard question, since we do not know just how old the Marcan account is. Both must go back surely to an Aramaic 'original'. When we come to study St Paul's doctrine of the Lord's Supper, I

---

[1] *The Kingdom of God and the Son of Man*, p. 326.

shall give reasons for believing that the Pauline version of the 'word' over the Cup, at least, is more original than the Marcan. More than that we probably cannot say, and even that is disputed.

What then shall we say of the twice-repeated formula, 'This do in remembrance of me'? If the shorter Western text of Luke be accepted,[1] as the critical fashion is nowadays, Paul is our only authority for the words. Can Jesus have actually used them?

Before answering that question let me say a word about Lietzmann's theory. Lietzmann detects the note of cultus in the use of ποιεῖτε, and finds parallels for the formula εἰς τὴν ἀνάμνησιν in 'the institution-records of ancient cult-fellowships'.[2] Hence he comes to the conclusion that what Paul 'received of the Lord' was 'the new conception of the Lord's Supper as a meal for the dead'.[3]

But surely it is quite unnecessary to search for parallels in pagan sources when Jewish parallels are available. 'The rich feast-tradition of Judaism', says Lohmeyer, 'is nothing else than a tradition εἰς ἀνάμνησιν. The idea emerges often and early in the Old Testament (e.g. Ex. 12.24-27). It is repeated in the blessing for the feast-day (which, moreover, is attached to the blessing over the wine at the Passover), "Praised be thou, O Lord our God . . . who hast given thy people Israel feast-days for joy and *for remembrance*" (Ber. 49*a*, 44).'[4]

This part of Lietzmann's theory, like other parts, is far from invulnerable. But does the Greek mean 'in remembrance of me'? C. A. Scott has argued that the words should be rendered 'with a view to recalling me'.[5] That is possible, and chimes in with what we shall see was probably the central significance of the Lord's Supper.

Did Jesus actually use the words? Mark does not record them. Did he take them for granted? This question will be examined later. Suffice it here to say that Paul's teachers at a very early date believed the Lord had used them—this is undoubtedly good evidence—and that whether Jesus uttered them or not, the command to repeat the meal is implicit in the eschatological utterance of Mark 14.25 (of which we catch an echo in I Cor. 11.26), i.e., if the words, 'This do,

---

[1] i.e. Luke 22.17–19*a*.   [2] I Kor. (*HNT*), p. 58.   [3] I Kor. (*HNT*), p. 58.
[4] *Theologische Rundschau* (1937), pp. 192–3.
[5] *Christianity according to St Paul*, p. 191.

etc.', are an interpretative addition, they only make explicit what was in Jesus' mind on the night of the betrayal. Fuller explanation must wait until we discuss Paul's conception of the Lord's Supper.

Appendix: GUARDED TRADITION

'The tradition of the apostles is guarded', says the writer of the Epistle to Diognetus somewhere about the middle of the second century. But it is probable that 'guarded tradition' played an important *rôle* in Christianity at an earlier date.

A priori, this seems likely. Among the Jews, apart from the scriptures, fixed and guarded oral tradition was the means for preserving the teaching of the great rabbis. We find a like process preserving the folk-songs of Israel: both words and music were handed down for centuries by uncultivated labourers with extraordinary accuracy. (In the absence of written and printed records men's memories were much more efficient.)

Now the early Christians depended greatly on the Old Testament. The New Testament was not yet in existence, nor was a new canon of scripture for that matter contemplated at all. Thus tradition was the great method, and it must have been guarded by the church as no tradition is guarded today.

If we seek evidence for this 'guarded tradition' in the early Christian literature, there is of course the emphatic witness of the Pastorals, with its call to 'guard the deposit' and to 'hold fast the pattern of sound words'; or again the allusion in Jude (verse 3) to 'the faith once delivered to the saints'.

But even in Paul's day it is probable that some attempt was made to fix and guard the Christian tradition—both doctrinal and moral. 'Hold the traditions which ye were taught whether by word or our epistle' says II Thess. 2.15. I Cor. 11.2 exhorts the Corinthians 'to hold fast the traditions even as I delivered them unto you'. Indeed, the two pieces of *paradosis* quoted in this letter—I Cor. 11.23 f. and 15.3 f.—probably represent examples of this guarded tradition, taught by catechists to converts when they became members of the church, or to missionaries when they received their commission.

One word more. To emphasize the place of 'guarded tradition' in the early church is not to deny that there was also much floating oral tradition. It seems to me, however, a weakness of the *Formgeschichte* school that they fail to recognize the place of guarded tradition in the primitive church, and tend to regard all tradition as floating and unfixed.

III · Pre-Pauline Formulae

LET US PASS NOW TO ANOTHER SIMILAR SORT OF PRE-PAULINE tradition discoverable in St Paul's epistles—what can be roughly described as 'Pre-Pauline Formulae and *Kerygma*'.

Such survivals are harder to detect; for Paul does not expressly label them as 'tradition'. We have to 'distil' such pre-Pauline elements out of the epistles. But we have certain criteria to help us in our search. To begin with, the literary form of the passage often, like Peter's Galilean accent, 'bewrays' it. The stylistic test is, however, far from infallible. The internal evidence of the suspected passage must be carefully examined. But if the content of the suspected passage discloses un-Pauline conceptions, then the inference will be strong that we are dealing with 'tradition', and not something struck for the first time in the Pauline mint. Absolutely conclusive proof is not to be expected: the reader must decide in each particular instance whether on a balance of probabilities the case is made out.

(i) We begin with Rom. 1.3–5:

> Paul, a servant of Jesus Christ, called to be an apostle, separated unto the gospel of God
> which he promised afore by his prophets in the holy scriptures concerning his son
> who was born of the seed of David according to the flesh
> who was declared to be the Son of God with power, according to the spirit of holiness by the resurrection of the dead; even Jesus Christ our Lord, etc. (RV).

Few will deny that even in their English dress these verses sound like 'a kind of potted creed'. The diction, and the careful parallelism of the phrases combine to give the passage a credal ring. Moreover,

24

we find here in the Greek that combination of participial and relative clauses which Norden has shown to be characteristic of the formulary style.

Here, however, I want to suggest that the traditional arrangement of this passage (found in AV and RV) is unsatisfactory. That arrangement gives us two relative clauses descriptive of the 'Son', namely:

1. 'Who was born of the seed of David according to the flesh'
2. 'Who was declared to be the Son of God with power according to the spirit of holiness by the resurrection of the dead, etc.'

Clause (2) on this arrangement is extraordinarily difficult. Three prepositional phrases are cluttered together, and it is very hard to know what precisely ἐν δυνάμει and κατὰ πνεῦμα ἁγιωσύνης signify. The suggested interpretations (see Sanday and Headlam, ad loc.) do not sound convincing.

Now the Peshitta presupposes a triadic division,[1] thus:

'Concerning his Son
1. Who was born of the seed of David according to the flesh
2. Who was appointed Son of God with power according to the Holy Spirit.
3. As a result of the resurrection of the dead Jesus Christ our Lord.'

This, it seems to me, gives better sense than the traditional arrangement. Clause (1) authenticates Jesus as the Messiah of Jewish prophecy. Clause (2) refers to the Baptism. By the descent of the Holy Spirit upon him he was 'appointed' (ὁρισθέντος, to be discussed in a moment) Son of God; πνεῦμα ἁγιωσύνης is a Hebraistic expression for πνεῦμα ἅγιον, and ἐν δυνάμει refers to his equipment with Messianic power at his Baptism. We think at once of the synoptic accounts of the Baptism, especially the reference to Psalm 2.7 ('Thou art my son; this day have I begotten thee,' cf. Luke 3.22), and of Peter's speech in Acts 10.38 ('how that God anointed him with the Holy Ghost and with power'—a probable reference to the Baptism).

---

[1] I owe this suggestion to T. W. Manson. The Syriac translated reads: 'Concerning his Son; who was born according to the flesh of the seed of David's house; and made known as Son of God with power and holy spirit; who rose from the house of the dead, even Jesus Messiah our Lord.'
This surely implies a triple division. 'Rose' would seem to suggest a third participle in the underlying Greek.

The third clause means 'Who as a result of (or after) the resurrection [became] Jesus Christ our Lord,' and this again chimes in with Acts 2.36 and Phil. 2.9 (itself probably pre-Pauline). The chief objection to this arrangement is the lack of a participle in Clause (3) corresponding to 'born' and 'appointed'; but I do not think this objection is decisive.

However, even if the traditional arrangement be preferred, I believe a strong case can be made out for the pre-Pauline character of our passage.

We have seen that the passage has all the marks of a creed. Let us pause now to examine the word ὁρισθέντος: its meaning is crucial for the interpretation of the passage. I do not think 'declared to be' (AV and RV) a proper rendering. The contemporary linguistic evidence we possess clearly favours the translation 'appointed' (Moffatt 'installed', Lietzmann 'bestellt'). The uncompounded ὁρίζω occurs nowhere else in Paul—which is perhaps significant. But in the two passages of Acts (10.42 and 17.31) where it occurs and in Ignatius (Eph. iii.2) 'appoint' is the obvious and natural rendering.[1] He who would maintain the traditional translation must bear the burden of linguistic proof.

Now consider what these verses say. According to the traditional arrangement, they describe Jesus as a real man who was acknowledged as Messiah (for primitive Christianity the descent from David was important as the guarantee that Jesus was the Messiah foretold in prophecy) and who after (or 'as a result of') the resurrection of the dead was appointed Son of God. This is not the Christological position of St Paul. Paul's doctrine—witness Rom. 8.3; I Cor. 10.4; II Cor. 8.9; Gal. 4.4—is incarnationist; this is adoptionist. In Rom. 1.3 ff. we learn of One who was a true man born of David's lineage whom God appointed Son of God after the resurrection. The resurrection is the birthday of the Son of God.

If we accept the triadic arrangement, we have still the clear suggestion of adoptionism. On this view the baptism is the birthday of the Son of God, and we have here something very like the Western text of Luke 3.22.

But there is another feature of the formula which leads us to

[1] Examples of the use of the verb with persons are rare. Moulton and Milligan quote nothing relevant.

suspect something pre-Pauline—the reference to the descent from the seed of David. At once there flashes into memory II Tim. 2.8, itself probably, as the commentators have noted, a 'semi-quotation from an early creed':[1] 'Remember Jesus Christ risen from the dead, of the seed of David.' We remember, too, not only the general belief in the Davidic descent of Jesus which crops up again and again in the New Testament, but also three semi-credal references in Ignatius to Jesus as 'born of the seed of David' (Smyrn. i.1; Eph. 18.2; Trall. ix.1). But why does Paul here introduce this reference at all? Is it one of his characteristic beliefs? Does he make great play with it elsewhere? On the contrary, he never mentions[2] it. May we not infer that the only reason for its inclusion here is that it stood in a pre-Pauline (and surely originally Palestinian) formula which was probably familiar to his addressees in Rome.[3]

Note. I should like to append authoritative support for this view from what was probably the last article from the pen of Hans Windisch ('Zur Christologie der Pastoralbriefe', *ZNTW* 34 (1935)). Windisch begins by disputing the view commonly held concerning the Christology of the Pastorals, i.e. that it is 'deutero-Pauline', namely, the doctrine of a pre-existent and glorified Christ with an admixture of Johannine and other elements.

Alongside some few expressions teaching Christ's pre-existence stand other passages with no suggestion of pre-existence—passages which reflect an older tradition of which echoes can be caught occasionally in St Paul's acknowledged epistles. He instances in the first place II Tim. 2.8. Two items from the evangelic tradition are here selected for emphasis: (1) the resurrection, (2) the generation from the seed of David. This selection is not accidental. These two items represent, Windisch contends, the two ἀρχαί, the beginnings of Christ's two modes of existence. 'There is presupposed a Christological *kerygma* (probably of Jewish-Christian origin) founded on the Old Testament. This *kerygma* is built on two main planks: (*a*) the man born of David's seed, therefore the Man-Messiah who was

---

[1] See Lock, *The Pastoral Epistles* (ICC), ad loc.

[2] Among the fixed formulae of the primitive Christology belongs also the idea, taken over by St Paul (Rom. 1.3), that Jesus was born of the seed of David; this was an indispensable antecedent of the future Messianic King.—Weiss, p. 123 (op. cit.).

[3] So C. H. Dodd, *Romans*, ad loc., K. Lake argues the existence of Adoptionist Christology in the Roman *Shepherd of Hermas* (see *Landmarks*, pp. 111 ff.).

born and appeared in accordance with Old Testament prophecy; (*b*) the man raised to divine honours.' After the death which he had to suffer like any other man, he was raised from the dead—here perhaps we should add 'according to the scriptures', as in I Cor. 15.3 f.

In proof of the existence of such a kerygmatic type, Windisch points to I Cor. 15.1, 4. But it appears, he observes, even more clearly in our passage, Rom. 1.3 ff. Here again we find the doctrine of the two existences, the two ἀρχαί. But this passage goes further than II Tim. 2.8. It describes the two modes of existence explicitly as κατὰ σάρκα and κατὰ πνεῦμα. 'The addition of these two phrases —as well as the use of the two significant verbs γενομένου and ὁρισθέντος—points decisively to a doctrine of the two existences.'

He concludes: 'As I think, Paul here employs the same two-existence Christological *kerygma* as in II Tim. 2.8. This *kerygma* was not created by Paul, but taken over from an older Jerusalem or Antioch tradition, a tradition which did not as yet know the doctrine of Christ's pre-existence.'

Which, although the method of approach is quite different, is much the same conclusion as I reached above.

(ii) We pass now to another passage in Romans where we scent something older than Paul—Rom. 10.8-9:
  'This is the word of faith (τὸ ῥῆμα τῆς πίστεως) which we preach, namely (ὅτι), if you confess with your mouth the word "Jesus is Lord" and believe in your heart that God raised him from the dead, you shall be saved.'
  (I translate W. H.'s text.)

When Paul declares salvation to consist in the confession of Jesus as Lord and the belief that God raised him from the dead, he is not defining salvation according to St Paul but reproducing common apostolic Christianity.

The introductory sentence prepares us to expect something from the common Christian *credo*. It is 'the word of faith'—or perhaps 'the formula which expresses faith'[1]—which forms the substance of

[1] C. A. Scott, *Christianity according to St Paul*, p. 119. He compares the use of ῥῆμα in Eph. 5.26.

28

the apostolic *kerygma*. The phrase means practically 'the gospel message'.

The content of this 'word' or 'formula' is twofold: a public confession 'Jesus is Lord'; and a heart-belief 'that God raised him from the dead'. (The words 'with your mouth' and 'in your heart' are from Deut. 30.11–14 which he has just cited.)

1. 'Jesus is Lord.' Paul's manner of quoting this confession here and elsewhere (I Cor. 12.3; Phil. 2.11; cf. II Cor. 4.5, 6; Acts 2.36, 19.5) makes it clear that he is quoting what was one of the oldest of Christian creeds, a creed that went back very far, perhaps indeed to the days after the resurrection. In all probability it was the pre-baptismal formula of confession of faith, baptism being at first in the name of the Lord. 'Jesus is Lord', is therefore as Sasse says, 'an old credal formula which bears all the marks of a genuine creed and should be viewed as a preparatory step to the later Christian confessions of faith'.[1]

2. 'And believe . . . that God raised him from the dead.'

Here again we are dealing with pre-Pauline Christianity. After our discussion of I Cor. 15.3 ff., it is superfluous to prove that belief in Christ as risen was the very keystone in the arch of the earliest Christian tradition. On that belief the Christian church was built. To say that Paul was not the first to preach 'Jesus and the resurrection' is to state the axiomatic.

But we can go further. Since this belief was cardinal in primitive Christianity, we should expect not only that it would bulk large in early Christian documents but also that it would be crystallized in certain semi-credal phrases.

'For Diaspora Judaism', writes Bousset, 'the idea of faith (in the sense of faith in the one God) lay at the very centre of religious life. The $\pi\rho\hat{\omega}\tau o\nu$ $\pi i\sigma\tau\epsilon\nu\sigma o\nu$ $\H{o}\tau\iota$ $\epsilon\hat{\iota}s$ $\H{\epsilon}\sigma\tau\iota\nu$ $\H{o}$ $\Theta\epsilon\acute{o}s$ became the characteristic shibboleth of Judaism in the Dispersion. But now the special distinguishing mark of the Christian fellowship became the confession of Jesus as Lord or the belief in the God who raised him from the dead.' This is altogether probable, and Bousset can therefore go on to say, 'Paul appears in his argumentations to take for granted an already formulated confession of faith in the Church: "If you confess with your mouth Jesus as Lord and believe in your

[1] *Mysterium Christi*, p. 93.

heart that God raised him from the dead you shall be saved." The formula', Bousset continues, ' "Believe in the God who raised Christ from the dead", may have been a piece of tradition when he got it.'[1]

When we consider the following passages, this conjecture seems well founded:

Rom. 4.24. Us who believe in him who raised Christ from the dead.

Rom. 8.11. The Spirit of him who raised Christ from the dead.

II Cor. 4.14. Knowing that he who raised Christ from the dead, etc.

Gal. 1.1. God the Father who raised Christ from the dead.

I Pet. 1.21. Who through him believe in God who raised him from the dead.

This coincidence of language (even clearer in the Greek where in every case the verb is ἐγείρειν, not ἀναστῆσαι, and the prepositional phrase ἐκ νεκρῶν (or ἐκ τῶν νεκρῶν) not ἀπὸ τῶν νεκρῶν) is surely not fortuitous.

We are warranted, therefore, in recognizing in Rom. 10.9 two palmary articles of faith in the pre-Pauline church—'Jesus is Lord' and 'Believe in the God who raised Christ from the dead'.

(iii) I should like here to mention and support a suggestion of Bultmann[2] that the pre-Pauline Christian tradition peeps out in Rom. 4.24–25.

24*b*. ' . . . Who believe (τοῖς πιστεύουσιν) on him that raised Jesus our Lord from the dead.

25. Who was delivered up for our trespasses and was raised for our justification.'

The words have, as Lietzmann has said,[3] 'almost the ring of a formulary confession of faith'. The marks of the formulary style are discernible in the combination of the relative and participial clauses (ἐπὶ τὸν ἐγείραντα ᾿Ιησοῦν τὸν Κύριον κτλ. . . . . ὃς παρεδόθη). There is clear *parallelismus membrorum*—

ὃς παρεδόθη διὰ τὰ παραπτώματα ἡμῶν
καὶ ἠγέρθη διὰ τήν δικαίωσιν ἡμῶν

---

[1] *Kyrios Christos*, p. 102.
[2] Made in conversation with the writer.   [3] Romans (*HNT*), ad loc.

And 24*b* probably echoes a pre-Pauline article of Christian faith (see discussion of Rom. 10.9).

Before we examine the internal evidence, one or two prolegomena are necessary.

Various evidences unite to show that before Paul there had been some theological reflection on the death of Jesus, some attempt to explain the *skandalon* of the Cross. The clearest bit of evidence, brief though it is, is the clause, 'Christ died for (ὑπέρ) our sins' in the pre-Pauline *paradosis* of I Cor. 15.3. The same 'for' (ὑπέρ) occurs also in the other piece of *paradosis* in I Cor. 11.24, 'This is my body which is for you' (ὑπὲρ ὑμῶν).

Moreover, *a priori* we should have expected that an explanation would be sought in the Old Testament scriptures—an expectation confirmed by the κατὰ τὰς γραφάς of I Cor. 15.3 ff.—and particularly in Isa. 53 (especially if Jesus had himself so tried to explain his vocation). That the earliest theologians did find the solution they were seeking in Deutero-Isaiah seems the natural explanation of the παῖς θεοῦ passages[1] in the early chapters of Acts behind which probably lies 'an original Aramaic tradition (whether written or oral) in which the Messiah was described unambiguously as the Servant of the Lord'.[2]

Let us return to Rom. 4.25. Altogether apart from the credal ring of the passage, the introductory τοῖς πιστεύουσιν leads us to expect something from the common Christian tradition. And there follows a carefully-worded expression of belief answering to all we have set forth above. 'Christ died for our sins' translated into the language of the Suffering Servant passage is 'who was delivered up for our trespasses' (cf. Isa. 53.12, LXX). But it was also foretold that 'by his knowledge shall my righteous servant *justify* many'. So the second line of the parallelism reads 'who was raised for our justification'.

We can strengthen our case by an appeal to παρεδόθη. We have already suggested that παρεδίδετο[3] in the pre-Pauline narrative of I Cor. 11.23 ff. means 'was (being) delivered up' (not betrayed) by

---

[1] Acts 3.13, 26; 4.27, 30; cf. Acts 8.32 ff.

[2] Rawlinson, *New Testament Doctrine of the Christ*, p. 241; Bousset, Bultmann, and Burkitt think the application of the Servant-conception to Jesus was the work of Hellenistic Christianity. Burkitt (*Christian Beginnings*, pp. 35–9) is well answered by Rawlinson (op. cit.).

[3] The introduction, 'The Lord Jesus the night in which he was delivered up' is part of the 'Paradigm', not Paul's work. See Dibelius, *From Tradition to Gospel*, pp. 48, 180.

31

Judas) in the sense of Isa. 53.12 (LXX). The same thought underlies our Lord's use of the word (Mark 9.31, 10.33, 14.41; Luke
24.7).[1] In short, the idea expressed by παρεδίδετο in I Cor. 11.23 is
pre-Pauline and shows that those who shaped the narrative (the
Christians of Damascus?) were even then seeking, like their Lord
before them, to interpret Christ's Passion in terms of the Suffering
Servant of the Lord.

I think, therefore, that we are entitled to find in Rom. 4.25 a
snatch of *kerygma* from the pre-Pauline Christian tradition.[2]

Note. A possible objection to this view is that δικαίωσις is a
characteristically Pauline word. Does not the term smack of Paul's
own doctrine of 'justification by faith'?

Apart from the fact that this particular word occurs only once
elsewhere in Paul (Rom. 5.18), I am disposed to question the
conventional view that this doctrine was Paul's *peculium*.

It is agreed that in Romans Paul often appeals to Christian beliefs
shared in common by the Roman church and himself. Must not the
doctrine of 'justification by faith' which bulks so large in this epistle
have been familiar to them?

Both the standard Old Testament proof-texts for the doctrine (Gen.
15.6 and Hab. 2.4) are probably common Christian *testimonia*.[3]

In Gal. 2.16 Paul can appeal to Peter on this very common
ground. 'Knowing that a man cannot be justified by the works of the
law, but only through faith in Jesus, we also put our trust in Jesus
Christ.' Let us give this passage its full weight: 'You and I, Cephas,'
says Paul, 'are at one in this doctrine of justification by faith. We
agree that a man is accepted by God not for his works of law but
for his faith in Christ.' (Cf. Peter's speech, Acts. 15.7–11.)

When we remember too that the germs of the doctrine are in the
gospels (Luke 18.10 ff. and Luke 15.11 ff.) we may well doubt the
commonly accepted view that this doctrine is stamped with the
Pauline hallmark.[4]

---

[1] See E. A. Abbott, *Paradosis*, pp. 3 f.
[2] I find that Weiss reckons Rom. 4.25 'among the doctrinal statements which St
Paul derived from the early Church'. He includes also I Thess. 5.10 and Gal. 1.4. See
History of Primitive Christianity, p. 104.
[3] See Harris, *Testimonies*, ad loc.
[4] Cf. Weiss, *History of Primitive Christianity*, p. 231. 'One always comes back to the
theory that these well-known controversial conceptions were not first created by Paul'.
Cf. G. Dix, *Jew and Greek*, 45, 'This is not a Pauline discovery.'

(iv) Faith, Hope, Love—A Primitive Christian Triad.

How many of us realize that 'Faith, hope, love' is probably a very primitive Christian triad and not the creation of St Paul?

Firmly linked, as it is, in our minds with the close of St Paul's sublime hymn in praise of love (I Cor. 13.13) we are reluctant to admit that this triad is not an inspired *ipse dixit*, an original collocation of the apostle himself. Yet several strands of evidence unite to prove that the triad is not Paul's own coinage, but a piece of pre-Pauline Christianity derived possibly from a saying of Jesus himself.

The triad is found not only in I Cor. 13.13, but also in I Thess. 1.3, 5.8; Rom. 5.1–5; Gal. 5.5–6; Col. 1.4–5; Eph. 4.2–5; Heb. 6.10–12, 10.22–24; I Pet. 1.3–8, 21–22, and once or twice in the Apostolic Fathers.

The following scheme shows how this triadic formula recurs, in various sequences, throughout early Christian literature.

I Thess. 1.3. Your work of faith and labour of love and patience of hope.

I Thess. 5.8. The breastplate of faith and love . . . a helmet, the hope of salvation.

Col. 1.4–5. Faith in Christ . . . love to all . . . the hope which is, etc.

Eph. 4.2–5. Forbearing one another in love . . . one hope of your calling . . . one Lord, one faith.

Heb. 6.10–12. And the love . . . the fulness of hope . . . through faith, etc.

I Pet. 1.3–8. A living hope . . . guarded through faith . . . whom having not seen, ye love.

I Pet. 1.21–22. So that your faith and hope . . . unto unfeigned love.

Heb. 10.22–24. Fulness of faith . . . the confession of our hope . . . unto love.

Gal. 5.5–6. By faith wait for the hope . . . through love.

I Cor. 13.13. And now abideth faith, hope, love.

Rom. 5.1–5. Justified by faith . . . the hope of the glory . . . because the love.

Barnabas i.4. Because great faith and love dwell in you in the hope.

Barnabas xi.8. In faith and love and hope for many.

Polycarp ad Phil. iii.2, 3. Into the faith given you ... when hope follows ... and love of God and Christ and neighbour goes before.

N.B. In the last five passages culled from the New Testament, the same sequence of the graces is observed by three different writers.

All this is surely not fortuitous. It strongly suggests that the triad in Paul is not his own creation, but something common and apostolic, perhaps a sort of compendium of the Christian life current in the early apostolic church.

Some incidental features in Paul's method of quoting the triad lend colour to this conjecture.

1. Consider how it crops up in I Cor. 13. Three points deserve notice. First, why does Paul drag in faith and hope at all at the end of his hymn in praise of love? The earlier verses of the chapter do not prepare us for their appearance here. The inference is that the mention of love suggested the other two members of what was already a traditional triad.

Second, Paul does not as a rule bracket faith and hope as of equal importance with love.

Third, the words 'these three', following the mention of 'faith, hope, love', suggest that it is a *familiar* triad. It is as if Paul says: 'Faith, hope, love—you know, the well-known three.'

2. Very significant is the almost tell-tale way in which Paul quotes the triad in I Thess. 5.8, 'Putting on the breastplate of faith and love, and for an helmet, the hope of salvation.'

The figure of the spiritual warrior and his panoply is, of course, old and Jewish. Compare Isa. 59.17, 'He put on righteousness as a breastplate, and an helmet of salvation upon his head.' (Cf. also Wisdom of Solomon 5.18.)

Now notice (in the Greek) the double genitive after 'breastplate' in I Thess. 5.8. The figure, to be perfect for Paul's purpose, would have named three pieces of armour—say, the breastplate of faith, the buckler of love, and the helmet of hope. Not finding the second piece of armour in the old metaphor, yet desiring to work in the three elements of his triad, Paul has to write, 'the breastplate of faith and love', and keep his second piece of armour for 'hope'.

But the phrase 'for an helmet, the hope of salvation' points to the same conclusion. The original figure spoke of 'a helmet of salvation' (as indeed we find it in Eph. 6.17). To complete the triad Paul had to work in 'hope'. He did so, quite patently, by writing 'the hope of salvation' and putting 'for an helmet' in apposition to this phrase.

In fine, we have found that Paul combines the old Jewish figure with the pre-Pauline Christian triad, 'Faith, hope, love', and that it is only with some difficulty that he achieves the combination.

Our last problem is this: Where, if St Paul did not invent the triad, did it originate?

Most scholars are content to call it traditional and speculate no further. But there is, in my judgment, some reason for thinking that the triad was inspired by a saying of our Lord.

Macarius, in one of his Homilies (xxxvii), has preserved a remarkable *agraphon* which I may translate: 'Hearing the Lord saying, Take care of *faith* and *hope* through which is begotten the *love* of God and of man which gives eternal life.' Is it rash to find in this uncanonical saying of the Lord the original of the triad?

We do not find anything in the synoptic gospels quite parallel to this saying. There ἀγάπη (love) occurs only twice. But its use in these two places (as Resch has pointed out), though probably quite accidental, is nevertheless interesting. In Luke 11.42 we find ἡ ἀγάπη τοῦ Θεοῦ, love in its Godward aspect, which answers almost exactly to ἡ φιλόθεος ἀγάπη, the phrase in Macarius. In Matt. 24.12 we find ἡ ἀγάπη τῶν πολλῶν, love in its manward aspect, which again recalls ἡ φιλάνθρωπος ἀγάπη in Macarius.

This is only a coincidence. I do not press it. But I do think that the twofold chain of evidence formed by (1) the recurrence of the triad in Paul, Peter, Hebrews, etc., and (2) the remarkable saying attributed by Macarius to the Lord, strongly suggests that this triadic formula is not only a bit of very early Christianity, but may very possibly be derived from a *logion* of Jesus.

IV · Pre-Pauline Christian Hymns

WE TURN NOW TO EXAMINE PRE-PAULINE CHRISTIAN HYMNS
to be found in Paul's letters.

But first of all one or two general observations about the beginnings of Christian hymnology.

> *A priori* we should expect that a religious movement which released such emotion . . . would find expression in song. Nor was the singing of praise to God a strange or unpractised art for the Christians of the first generation. Behind them lay an ancient habit of praise. From temple and from synagogue the strains of the Psalms had been rising to God for generations.[1]

The earliest hymn-book of the Christian church was the Jewish Psalter. The Christians, doubtless, read into these Jewish hymns new and nobler meanings, finding in the Messianic psalms prefigurements and prophecies of Jesus the Christ. Very soon, however, they must have begun to make hymns of their own in which they could give unfettered expression to the new hope that was in them. 'A great and wonderful new world of truth had swum into the ken of those who had learned of Christ. New springs of emotion had been unsealed. The old channels were not sufficient. New conduits had to be created. A new song had to be found.'[2]

In the year AD 111 Pliny wrote his famous rescript to Trajan about the Christians. In it he told his emperor that the Christians 'were wont to meet on a fixed day before dawn, and sing by turns (*invicem:* probably antiphonal singing) a hymn to Christ as to a god' (Pliny, Epp. x.96).

But the Christians were singing hymns some fifty years earlier.

[1] A. B. Macdonald, *Christian Worship in the Primitive Church*, p. 112.
[2] Millar Patrick, *Story of the Church's Song*, p. 17.

36

'When you meet together', Paul writes to the Corinthians (I Cor. 14.26), 'each contributes something—a sacred song ($\psi\alpha\lambda\mu\acute{o}\nu$), a lesson, a tongue, an interpretation.' Possibly $\psi\alpha\lambda\mu\acute{o}s$ denotes an unpremeditated hymn born in the spiritual exaltation of the moment; possibly it is an Old Testament psalm Christianly interpreted (see Acts 4.24 f.), 'Teach and train one another', Paul counsels the Colossians (3.16), 'with psalms, and hymns, and spiritual songs.'[1] Such references not only prove the existence of early Christian hymns, but also suggest their 'setting in the life' of the early church.

Of the beginnings of Christian hymnology there are scattered traces in the New Testament, the canticles of Luke, for example. These are Jewish in colouring (the *Magnificat* being patterned on Hannah's Song in I Sam. 2.1–10), and typify the eschatological hymn which celebrates future events as though they had already happened.

Then there are the stately hymnodic chants of praise in the Apocalypse (Rev. 4.11; 5.9–10, 12–13; 11.17 f.; 15.3–4; 19.6–8). Some are perhaps pre-Christian, but others are probably 'new songs', and though the Apocalypse represents them as sung by the heavenly choirs, we may suppose that hymns like these must have been used in earthly Christian worship at the time when the Apocalypse was written.

Once again, there are embedded in the Pastoral epistles one or two passages which are almost certainly fragments of early Christian hymns. The best example is I Tim. 3.16. Cf. II Tim. 2.11–13 and Titus 3.4–7. Such passages have more of the character of *carmina Christi* than the Lucan canticles or the chants of the Apocalypse.

We turn to the genuine epistles of St Paul. Can we detect in them any fragments of early Christian hymns?

All such detection must be, to some degree, speculative. We have no infallible criteria enabling us to pronounce such and such a passage a hymn in the strictest sense of the word, i.e. something sung by a Christian congregation as an act of worship. A metrical test is impossible: metrical verse in Christian hymnology came much later (e.g. P. Oxy, 1786, contains a Christian hymn of the third century, written in anapaestic metre, and complete with musical notes). Nevertheless, there are certain marks or traits which we may

[1] Cf. Eph. 5.19 and Acts 16.25.

37

expect in any hypothetical hymn: a certain rhythmical quality; correspondence between words and phrases; *parallelismus membrorum*; perhaps clearly-defined strophes; homoioteleuton, etc. These are stylistic tests. Yet even if a particular passage satisfies any or all of them, we may not lightly assume that we have unearthed a pre-Pauline hymn in Paul's epistles. St Paul, when he 'took fire', could produce exalted prose-poetry almost *currente calamo*—witness I Cor. 13 and Rom. 8.31 ff.—prose-poetry possessing many of the features of a carefully-composed hymn. In such cases we must examine the internal evidence. For this reason I reject David Smith's suggestion[1] that Rom. 6.8–10 is an earlier Christian hymn. Here are rhythm and parallelism, even homoioteleuton. But there is nothing in the contents to show that the passage is not the elevated argumentation of St Paul himself. Cf. also Rom. 13.11–12.

There are two passages in St Paul's epistles where, I think, we can confidently 'diagnose' pre-Pauline Christian hymns. They are Eph. 5.14 and Phil. 2.6–11. To them we must now turn.

(*a*) Eph. 5.14

> διὸ λέγει
> ἔγειραι ὁ καθεύδων
> καὶ ἀνάστα ἐκ τῶν νεκρῶν
> καὶ ἐπιφαύσει ὁ Χριστός
> [v. l. ἐπιφαύσει].

> Wherefore it (or he) says,
> Wake up, O Sleeper,
> and rise from the dead
> and the Christ will shine upon you.

The context shows that the verse is an appeal to 'wake up' out of the pagan state of sin described in the twofold metaphor of sleep and death, with the added promise that the Christ will then shine upon the sinner with the saving light of his truth.

The introductory formula, διὸ λέγει, leads us to expect a citation of scripture.

1. It is not a garbled quotation of Isa. 60.1, 'Arise, shine; for thy light is come, and the glory of the Lord is risen upon thee.' The

---

[1] *The Life and Letters of St Paul*, p. 411.

superficial resemblance between the two passages is counter-balanced by decisive differences.

2. To regard it as a bit of a lost Jewish apocalypse is to explain *obscurum per obscurius.*

3. Nor is Resch's attempt to prove it an *agraphon* any more successful.

4. The one theory which fits the facts is that it is an early (pre-Pauline) Christian baptismal hymn. That it is a hymn seems clear.

(*a*) διὸ λέγει indicates an express citation (sc. ὁ κύριος). The solemn words chanted at baptism might well have been set on a level with Old Testament scripture and introduced with a similar formula.

(*b*) The words fall easily and naturally into a three-lined rhythmic division. There is a swinging trochaic rhythm in the Greek, and homoioteleuton in the first two lines.

(*c*) The verse has the cult-style of the invocational appeal. Commentators rightly cite as a parallel the hymn from the Attis mysteries preserved in Apuleius:

> ἐκ τυμπάνου βέβρωκα
> ἐκ κυμβάλου πέπωκα
> γέγονα μύστης Ἄττεως.

(*d*) The atmosphere of the verse is baptismal. Cf. Rom. 6.4. The suggestion that the hymn in some way commemorates the descent into Hades seems inept. The hymn exactly suits the moment of baptism: As the convert rises from the baptismal wave—fit symbol of burial and death with the Lord with whom he is now united—the onlooking congregation break out into this hymn of exhortation. If this be so, 'Paul could take it for granted that everyone would know it, and also that it would carry associations of a peculiarly solemn kind. The convert rising from the baptismal wave in which he has washed away his sins is welcome into the new life. Christ will henceforth shine upon him and renew him.'[1]

(*b*) Phil. 2.6–11

The second example of a pre-Pauline Christian hymn embedded in St Paul's epistles is Phil. 2.6–11, the so-called *kenosis* passage.

---

[1] E. F. Scott, *Ephesians* (MNTC), ad loc.

Few passages in the New Testament have claimed more critical ink than this, and the exegesis of details and of the whole has been much disputed. Nevertheless, I believe that by using the clues furnished by recent research, we can reach a satisfactory explanation of this *crux interpretum*.

It is a pre-Pauline Jewish Christian hymn. Its theme is Jesus, the Second Adam, who conquering the temptation to which the First Adam fell, chose the *rôle* of the Suffering Servant and for his obedience unto death was highly exalted by God, and made 'Lord' of the whole cosmos.

It is a hymn. Lohmeyer's strophic arrangement of it,[1] which seems certainly the best, makes this clear:

1. ὃς ἐν μορφῇ θεοῦ ὑπάρχων
   οὐχ ἁρπαγμὸν ἡγήσατο
   τὸ εἶναι ἴσα θεῷ,

2. ἀλλ' ἑαυτὸν ἐκένωσε
   μορφὴν δούλου λαβών
   ἐν ὁμοιώματι ἀνθρώπων γενόμενος

3. καὶ σχήματι εὑρεθεὶς ὡς ἄνθρωπος
   ἐταπείνωσεν ἑαυτόν
   γενόμενος ὑπήκοος μέχρι θανάτου
                    [θανάτου δὲ σταυροῦ][2]

4. διὸ καὶ ὁ Θεὸς αὐτὸν ὑπερύψωσε
   καὶ ἐχαρίσατο αὐτῷ τὸ ὄνομα
   τὸ ὑπὲρ πᾶν ὄνομα

5. ἵνα ἐν τῷ ὀνόματι Ἰησοῦ
   πᾶν γόνυ κάμψῃ
   ἐπουρανίων καὶ ἐπιγείων καὶ καταχθονίων

6. καὶ πᾶσα γλῶσσα ἐξομολογήσηται
   ὅτι κύριος Ἰησοῦς Χριστὸς
   εἰς δόξαν Θεοῦ πατρός.

[1] *An die Philipper* (Meyer), ad loc.
[2] Probably a Pauline gloss. It mars the rhythm, and is moreover entirely in Paul's manner.

Have the same disposition among yourselves as you [have] in [your communion with] Christ Jesus:

1. Who being in God's *image*
   Did not consider equality with God
   Something to be seized.

2. Nay, he *poured himself out*
   Taking *servant's* form
   Becoming in men's likeness.

3. And being found in fashion as man
   He *humbled* himself
   Becoming obedient *unto death*
       (and that a cross-death!)

4. Therefore God also *highly exalted* him
   And conferred on him the name—
   The name above every name.

5. That at the name of Jesus
   Every knee might bow
   Of beings in heaven, on earth, and in
       the nether-world.

6. And every tongue confess,
   'Jesus Christ is Lord'
   To the glory of God the Father.

The artistic structure of the section is unmistakable. There are six strophes of three lines each: the first three describe the humiliation, the second three the exaltation of Christ. The style is rhythmical. There is careful parallelism of phrases. The order of the words is scarcely that of epistolary prose. Several phrases—τὸ εἶναι ἴσα θεῷ, τὸ ὄνομα τὸ ὑπὲρ πᾶν ὄνομα, εἰς δόξαν θεοῦ πατρός as terse as any formula. The style of the whole is solemn, stately, liturgical; and it ends with a rhetorical clause.[1]

Here, then, whether Paul's work or not, is a complete and carefully-built hymn.

---

[1] Further points in Lohmeyer, *Phil.* ad loc.

The context seems to confirm this. The passage stands in the middle of a hortatory section which begins at 1.27 and is resumed at 2.12. That is, the 'hymn' plainly interrupts the flow of the *paraenesis*: it is like a 'purple patch' stitched into the fabric of the exhortation.

When we examine the diction, we are struck at once by its un-Pauline features. Three words—ἁρπαγμός, ὑπερυψοῦν and καταχθόνιος —are *hapax legomena* not merely in Paul, but in the whole New Testament. μορφή is not found elsewhere in Paul. The apostle uses κενοῦν four times elsewhere in his writings, always in the sense 'make void', which certainly will not do here. Nowhere else does he use the precise form ἐν ὀνόματι Ἰησοῦ.

Further, there is a good deal of evidence (gathered by Loh-meyer)[1] to suggest that the hymn, though originally written in Greek, had an author whose mother-tongue was Aramaic: the participial style which is a familiar feature of Semitic hymnodical prayer-speech; the use of participles not in apposition to the main verb, but to denote progress of action ('only in Semitic speech can a finite verb be continued by a participle'); three-stress lines; and un-Greek phrases like εὑρεθεὶς ὡς ἄνθρωπος (cf. Gal. 2.17).

When we turn to the internal evidence, we look in vain for characteristically Pauline ideas. This is not Paul's doctrine of redemption: here humanity is not *redeemed*, but *subjected* to the new κύριος. Nothing is said of the resurrection of Jesus, and mention of this is surely determinative for St Paul. Instead, the emphasis —as in Hebrews—is on the *exaltation* (ὑπερύψωσε αὐτόν). Finally, the hymn depicts Jesus as 'Lord' not of the *church* but of the *cosmos*.

This evidence is, I believe, sufficient to warrant us finding here a pre-Pauline Jewish Christian hymn. If we ask whence Paul derived it, we can only speculate. Lohmeyer's suggestion that the hymn was part of the Eucharistic liturgy of the Palestinian church does not seem probable. The notes we should expect to hear—redemption, the new covenant, the parousia—are lacking. Perhaps it is safest to surmise that he found it in the churches of Syria where he spent a good deal of his life as a Christian when not engaged on missionary work. There, as we know, was a large Jewish population: Antioch was indeed a home-from-home for Hellenistic Jews.

[1] Lohmeyer, *Kyrios Jesus*, pp. 8 ff.

Let us turn to the interpretation of the hymn. Two conceptions supply the key—that of the two Adams, and that of the Suffering Servant (Isa. 52.13–ch. 53).

'Who being in the μορφή of God.' What is the sense of μορφή? Older exegetes (like Gifford) gave the word the philosophical connotation it had in Plato and Aristotle—as if Paul writing occasional letters from prison used language with the exactitude of a trained philosopher! Others, rightly rejecting such preciosity, held that the word simply meant 'nature' in a general sort of way.

But if μορφή here has the sense 'image', at once we get a clue to what follows. Now there is evidence that μορφή can translate the Aramaic word for 'image'.[1]

That meaning fits our passage like a glove—

> Who being in God's image
> Did not consider equality with God
> Something to be seized—

There is a clear reference to the Genesis story of the First Adam's fall. τὸ εἶναι ἴσα θεῷ echoes *'eritis sicut dei'*. The Second Adam might have conceived the senseless project of seizing by force (ἁρπαγμός = *res rapienda*) the equality with God he did not as yet possess, but conquering this temptation to which the First Adam fell, he chose the way of obedience unto death.

The second conception is that of the Suffering Servant of the Lord (the interpretation of Jesus' death in terms of this conception we have already seen to be pre-Pauline. See pp. 29 f. *supra* for discussion of Rom. 4.24–25). The echoes from Deutero-Isaiah are too many to be fortuitous. Obviously stanzas 4 and 5 reflect Isa. 45.23. But there are several echoes of Isa. 52.13–ch. 53. Behind μορφὴν δούλου λαβών stands probably the figure of the Servant. ἑαυτὸν ἐκένωσε refers to Isa. 53.12[2] ('because he poured out his soul unto death.' But cf. LXX); and the phrase means simply that he poured himself out, like water from a vase, in utter self-sacrifice.

---

[1] See J. Héring, *Recherches Théologiques* (1) 1936, pp. 12–25. The Peshitta here (i.e. in Phil. 2.6) renders μορφή by 'demoutha'. In Daniel 3.9 'tsalma' is rendered in the LXX by μορφή. Cf. the Hebrew of Gen. 1.26 with the LXX. There is definite evidence of the equivalence of μορφή and εἰκών, as renderings of the Aramaic 'demoutha' or 'tsalma'.

[2] ἐκκενοῦν is used in three places in the LXX to render the Piel of 'ārāh, and the Hiphil of the same verb is used in Isa. 53.12, which might therefore have been translated ἐξεκένωσεν τὴν ψυχήν αὐτοῦ εἰς θάνατον. See Dodd, *JTS*, July 1938.

ἐταπείνωσεν ἑαυτόν in stanza 3 surely reflects Isa. 53.7 (RV 'He was oppressed, yet he *humbled* himself.' Cf. LXX. ἐν τῇ ταπεινώσει αὐτοῦ). If Christ was obedient μέχρι θανάτου, the Servant was led away εἰς θάνατον (Isa. 53.8, LXX). And if Christ was 'highly exalted', we recall that Isa. 52.13 prophesies that the Servant 'shall be exalted (LXX ὑψωθήσεται) and glorified exceedingly'.

If our whole theory be sound, then Paul's conception of Christ as the Second Adam (Rom. 5.12–21; I Cor. 15.45–49) goes back to the pre-Pauline Christian tradition.

V · 'Words of the Lord'

ANOTHER PROOF OF ST PAUL'S DEPENDENCE ON THE PRE-Pauline Christian tradition appears in the 'Words of the Lord' quoted or echoed in his epistles. These Paul must have received from those who were 'in Christ' before him.

There are more of these 'Words' than is commonly supposed. How trite is the remark that Paul knew little of the sayings of Jesus and therefore took no account of them! No one who has carefully examined Paul's exhortations will be guilty of such a snap-judgment.

On the other hand, certain scholars in their eagerness to prove Paul's knowledge of the historic Jesus, make the opposite mistake, discovering reminiscences of Jesus' words where only a *tour de force* of pious imagination could detect them. Against both errors we must be on our guard.

Before we study the 'Words' themselves, let me say something of the use made of these 'Words of the Lord' in the apostolic age.

First, the apostolic writers use the sayings of Jesus not to buttress a point of doctrine or *kerygma* but for practical and paraenetic purposes. Paul's own usage proves this. Bating I Thess. 4.15 f. (a doubtful exception, as we shall see), he refers to 'Words of the Lord' invariably in order to decide practical everyday Christian problems (e.g. marriage and the care of missionaries); or he weaves them into the fabric of his exhortations.

Second, it would seem that very early collections of these 'Words' were made for the use of missionaries and teachers. We find sporadic traces of such collections in I Clement (xiii.2), Polycarp to the Philippians (ii.3) and the Didache (i.3).

Third, the 'Words' were introduced in two different ways. They were either explicitly cited as 'Words of the Lord' or they were included tacitly in the exhortations.

In the former case some formula of quotation introduces them, as 'Remember the words of the Lord Jesus' (I Clem. xlvi.7; cf. Acts 20.35).

In the latter case no indication is given that a 'Word' is to follow. A good example, outside of Paul, of this tacit quotation of a saying of Jesus is James 5.12. Thus, genuine sayings of Jesus lie cheek by jowl with other words of exhortation. We rely on our knowledge of Jesus' teaching preserved in the synoptic tradition to enable us to detect echoes of it in the apostolic writers. It is possible, therefore, that there may be other sayings of Jesus lying unidentified in the pages of Paul and other apostolic authors.

With these prolegomena let us examine the traces of Jesus' 'Words' discernible in St Paul's epistles.

I Cor. 7.10. 'But unto the married I give charge, yea not I but the Lord, that the wife depart not from her husband . . . and that the husband leave not his wife.' Here we have not the *ipsissima verba* but the substance of the Lord's ruling (Matt. 19.6; Mark 10.9; Luke 16.18). Paul knew that Jesus had pronounced on the indissolubility of marriage.

I Cor. 9.14. 'Even so did the Lord ordain that they which proclaim the gospel should live of the gospel.' The saying referred to is probably 'The labourer is worthy of his hire' (Luke 10.7 = Matt. 10.10).[1] Like I Cor. 7.10, this verse gives the substance of the Lord's 'Word'. From very early days, evidently, Christian missionaries justified their claim to maintenance by an appeal to something Jesus had said.

I Cor. 11.23 ff. is the narrative of the Lord's Supper already considered. Here Jesus' actual words are quoted.

The fourth 'Word' is not so certain or simple (I Thess. 4.15 f.). The actual 'Word' is possibly to be found in verse 16, 'For the Lord himself shall descend from heaven, with a shout, with the voice of the archangel, and with the trump of God.' Mark 13.26 f. (and parallels) *may* be the 'Word' intended. But perhaps Schweitzer is right in regarding the 'Word' here as a revelation of Christ made to Paul through the Spirit.[2]

Lastly, here should be included the 'Word' in Acts 20.35. Since

---

[1] Cited as scripture in I Tim. 5.18.
[2] *The Mysticism of Paul the Apostle*, p. 174.

Luke was probably present on this occasion, and since this speech at Miletus is the most Pauline of all the speeches which the writer of Acts puts in Paul's mouth,[1] I see no reason for doubting that Paul did quote his Master's saying, 'It is more blessed to give than to receive', to the Ephesian elders. Although the *logion* has no place in the synoptic tradition, Clement of Rome probably echoes it (I Clem. 2.1), and we have no grounds for doubting its genuineness.

This completes the list of explicit references to 'Words of the Lord' in Paul.

More numerous are the sayings of Jesus included in the exhortations. Occasionally these are proper citations, oftener they are echoes and silent adaptations of Jesus' teaching.

Let us choose two hortatory sections from the epistles, and go through them picking out the echoes of the sayings of Jesus, and commenting briefly on them.

First, Romans, chapters 12–14.

12.14. 'Bless them that persecute you; bless and curse not.' Surely an echo of Matt. 5.44 (= Luke 6.28). We compare Did. i.3,' Bless those that curse you.' Moreover, in Rom. 12.14 Paul changes his construction from participle to imperative (the participle appears again in the next sentence)—a fact which suggests that he employs borrowed words and does not trouble to adapt them to their grammatical context.

12.17. 'Render to no man evil for evil.' Cf. Matt. 5.39 ff.; I Thess. 5.15; and I Pet. 3.9. Not a citation of any synoptic word, but a probable echo of Christ's teaching.

12.21. 'Be not overcome of evil, but overcome evil with good.' An epitome of Jesus' teaching about 'non-resistance'.

Now turn to chapter 13.

13.7. 'Render to all their dues: tribute to whom tribute is due, etc.' Is it conceivable that the writer of these words had never heard of the reply made by One whom the Pharisees tried to 'trap in his talk'? Cf. Mark 12.13–17 = Matt. 22.15–22 = Luke 20.20–26.

13.8–10. 'Owe no man anything, save to love one another: for he that loveth his neighbour hath fulfilled the law. For this, Thou shalt not commit adultery, Thou shalt not kill, Thou shalt not steal, Thou shalt not covet, and if there be any other commandment,

---

[1] See, e.g., *Cambridge Biblical Essays*, p. 401.

it is summed up in this word, namely, Thou shalt love thy neighbour as thyself. Love worketh no ill to his neighbour: love, therefore, is the fulfilment of the law.' (Cf. Mark 12.28–34 = Matt.
22.34–40 = Luke 10.25–28.) Possibly this way of summarizing the
Law was not unknown to the rabbis; but who will question that the
command to 'owe no man anything save the debt of mutual love',
coupled with the summing-up of the Decalogue in the great twin-
precept of love to God and love to man, took its inspiration and
origin from Jesus?

We pass to chapter 14.

First, we note Paul's strictures against 'judging' (verses 3, 4, 10,
and 13). 'But thou, why dost thou judge thy brother?' asks Paul.
'Judge not that ye be not judged', commands his Master (Matt.
7.1 = Luke 6.37).

Then Paul goes on: 'Let us not, therefore, judge one another any
more: but judge ye this rather, that no one put a stumbling-block
(πρόσκομμα) in his brother's way or an occasion of falling (σκάνδαλον).'
It seems very likely that Paul's thought and language are inspired by
the Lord's stern words about 'offences' (Matt. 18.6–9; Mark
9.42–48; Luke 17.1–2). 'σκάνδαλον is not a good or usual Greek
word, and the very fact that Paul uses it here suggests that he knew
it in the tradition of the sayings of Jesus.'[1]

14.14. 'I know and am persuaded in the Lord Jesus that nothing
is unclean of itself, etc.' Hard on top of the warning against σκάνδαλα
comes another exhortation of whose truth Paul is 'persuaded in the
Lord Jesus'. That persuasion very possibly goes back to some words
of Jesus in which he repealed at one stroke the whole conception of
ceremonial impurity (Mark 7.15; Matt. 15.11), and made religion
inward, spiritual, and free.

14.17. 'For the kingdom of God is not eating and drinking, but
righteousness, and peace, and joy in the Holy Ghost.' The kingdom
of God, says Paul in effect, is within you: it is 'inward peace and
inward might'. 'The Apostle's description of the kingdom of God
reads like a brief summary of its description in the same Sermon on
the Mount; the righteousness, peace, and joy which formed the
contents of the Kingdom in the Apostle's conception are found side
by side in the Saviour's Beatitudes.'[2]

---

[1] Dodd, *Romans*, ad loc. [2] Knowling, *Witness of the Epistles*, p. 312.

There are too many echoes and adaptations of the teaching of Jesus in these three chapters of Romans to put it all down to the 'nicest coincidences of sentiment' between Paul and his Master. The apostle shows clear knowledge both of the words and the essential spirit of Christ's teaching. The Pauline ethic here is saturated with the ethic of his Lord.

Let us pass now to I Thess. 4–5.

The exhortation begins with a warning against uncleanness, which Paul clinches at.

4.8. 'Therefore he that rejecteth (ὁ ἀθετῶν), rejecteth not man, but God who giveth his Holy Spirit unto you.' This sentence recalls, both in its thought and its use of ἀθετεῖν.

Luke 10.16. 'He that rejecteth you, rejecteth me; and he that rejecteth me rejecteth him that sent me.'

4.9*b*. 'For ye yourselves are taught of God to love one another', catches the essential spirit of Jesus' teaching.

4.16 is the 'Word' already discussed.

5.2–3. 'For you yourselves know that the day of the Lord so *cometh as a thief* in the night. When they are saying, Peace and safety, then sudden destruction cometh upon them, *as travail* upon a woman with child; and they shall in no wise escape.'

Here are several distinct echoes of apocalyptic sayings found on the lips of Jesus. Cf. Luke 12.39 and 21.34.

5.6. 'So then let us not sleep, as do the rest, but let us watch and be sober,' is not unlike Matt. 24.42, 'Watch, therefore, etc.'

5.8 contains the primitive Christian triad possibly based on an *agraphon* of Jesus.

5.13. 'Be at peace among yourselves,' is almost exactly paralleled in Jesus' words in Mark 9.50. Cf. Rom. 12.18.

5.15. 'See that none render unto any one evil for evil,' resembles closely the 'non-resistance' saying of Rom. 12.14, 17, already discussed.

Again we see Paul's exhortation permeated with the ethical teaching of Jesus. It is true that none of the parallels exactly reproduces a saying of Jesus as it is preserved in the synoptic gospels. But then Paul was not in a position to copy verbatim from the Synoptists! It is not so much odd echoes of particular *logia*, but repeated evidences that Paul had appropriated the essential principles of

Christ's ethic, which compel us to believe that the tradition of Jesus' teaching was familiar to him.

These examples do not exhaust the list of echoes and silent adaptations of Christ's sayings in Paul. There are others—for example:

Rom. 16.19. 'I would have you wise unto that which is good, and simple (ἀκεραίους) unto that which is evil' which is very reminiscent of Christ's word (Matt. 10.16) about serpents and doves. (The rare adjective, ἀκέραιος, 'simple', 'harmless', 'innocent', is common to both.)

Or I Cor. 13.2. 'If I have all faith so as to remove mountains.' Doubtless, 'removing mountains' was a current cliché among the rabbis for doing the impossible. Paul's connection of it with 'faith' suggests that he knew the Lord's saying (Mark 11.23 = Matt. 21.21).

Or Phil. 4.6, μηδὲν μεριμνᾶτε which reads like a reminiscence of Matt. 6.25 (Luke 12.22).

Did Paul know the Lord's Prayer? It is often said that, if he did, he shows no knowledge of it. I want merely to throw out the suggestion that there may be three echoes of it in the epistles:

1. Rom. 8.15. 'But ye received the spirit of adoption whereby we cry Abba, Father' ('Αββᾶ ὁ πατήρ). Cf. Gal. 4.6.

How came the Aramaic expression *Abba* to be used in letters sent to Romans and Galatians? The likeliest explanation is that it had been hallowed by liturgical use in the Lord's Prayer, and, like *Marana tha*, was taken over as it stood. Gentile converts naturally added the explanatory ὁ πατήρ. I Pet. 1.17, 'If ye call on him as Father', is probably to be explained in the same way. I am disposed to accept Zahn's conjecture,[1] that the phrase, 'whereby we cry *Abba*, Father,' refers to the corporate recitation of the *Paternoster* (Lucan form, presumably) by the newly baptized as the first exercise of their Christian privileges.

2. Col. 3.13. 'Forbearing one another and forgiving each other, if any man have a complaint against any; even as the Lord forgave you, so also do ye.' The whole thought of the passage recalls the petition in the Lord's Prayer, 'Forgive us our debts as we also forgive our debtors'. 'We can hardly doubt, with a verse like this

[1] *Brief des P. an die Römer* [1910], p. 395.

before us, that it [the Lord's Prayer] was familiar to him. He gives us, however, the other side of the petition in the prayer.'[1]

3. II Thess. 3.3. 'But the Lord is faithful who shall stablish you, and guard you from the evil one' (καὶ φυλάξει ἀπὸ τοῦ πονηροῦ). The language is very reminiscent of the petition in the Lord's Prayer (Matt. 6.13, ἀλλὰ ῥῦσαι ἀπὸ τοῦ πονηροῦ). The use of φυλάσσειν instead of ῥύεσθαι may be due to the fact that the latter verb occurs in the preceding verse (II Thess. 3.2). Cf. II Tim. 4.18.

To sum up: Paul had certainly a store of 'Words of the Lord' or 'Directions of the Lord'. This is proved by

(*a*) His explicit allusions to such 'Words'.

(*b*) His tacit use of sayings of Jesus in his exhortations.

(*c*) The saturation of his ethic by the ethic of his Master.

(*d*) Such a remark as I Cor. 7.25, 'Now concerning virgins, I have no commandment of the Lord.' He had, therefore, a number of such 'commandments' from which dominical rulings, like I Cor. 7.10 and 9.14, were derived. Amongst these directions he looked in vain for one about 'virgins', and 'we may almost hear his tone of regret as he confirms this lack'.[2] Now, all Paul's express references to 'Words of the Lord' occur in I Corinthians. This is significant. It is 'the only letter in which a number of practical questions affecting the life and organization of the church were dealt with by St Paul at the request of his converts. If more of such inquiries had been preserved in documents (for the situation must have been common), it is almost certain that we should have found numerous additional references to definite instructions of Jesus.'[3]

Were these 'Words' scribbled down on a bit of papyrus, or were they committed to memory? Possibly the latter is the better explanation: oriental memories—and especially the memory of one who had had a rabbinical training—were extraordinarily retentive. From whom did Paul get these 'Words'? We can only guess. Peter, Luke, Barnabas, could all have supplied him with them. What is certain is that Paul did have a knowledge of such 'Words'; and this knowledge is yet another evidence of his debt to the pre-Pauline Christian tradition.

[1] E. F. Scott, *Colossians*, ad loc.
[2] Dibelius, *From Tradition to Gospel*, p. 242.
[3] H. A. A. Kennedy, *The Theology of the Epistles*, p. 103.

VI · The Paraenetic Tradition

Paraenesis MEANS EXHORTATION, OR RATHER 'MORAL INSTRUCtion with a dash of exhortation'.

There circulated in the early church a paraenetic as well as a doctrinal tradition. The paraenetic tradition consisted of a mass of moral instructions which the apostolic missioners delivered to their converts for their guidance in the manifold problems of daily living. That tradition was pre-Pauline (indeed, in origin, pre-Christian) and Paul, in using it, shows his dependence upon the praxis of pre-Pauline Christianity.

These assertions must now be substantiated.

Every reader of the apostle knows that, after rounding off his doctrinal exposition, Paul often writes 'a word of exhortation'. This, generally speaking, is a collection of moral precepts which often are not obviously relevant to the particular circumstances of the church which he addresses. Further, the style of this exhortation is usually different from that of Paul's characteristic writing. Instead of long, sustained sentences, we find brief, gnomic precepts enunciating general rules. Recent investigation[1] has shown that what we have here is not Paul's own attempt to frame a code of everyday ethics, but traditional materials which the early Christian missioners transmitted to their converts.

The doctrinal tradition of the early church is known to us, in part at least, from I Cor. 15.3 ff. But certain passages indicate that Paul transmitted an ethical tradition also to his churches. They received —to use rabbinical terms—a Christian Halakha (i.e. tradition of rules for conduct) as well as a Christian Haggada (tradition of historical and theological material).

References to this tradition occur in I Thess. 4.1, where Paul

[1] See Dibelius, I Thess.[3] (*HNT*), pp. 19, 20.

declares 'You received (παρελάβετε) from us how you ought to walk' (περιπατεῖν: in the ethical sense), and in II Thess. 3.6, 'Withdraw yourselves from every brother that walketh disorderly and not after the tradition they received of us' (Paul explicitly refers to a *paradosis*). Cf. Rom. 6.17, 16.17; I Cor. 4.17 and I Cor. 11.2.

This 'tradition' has nothing to do with 'doctrine' as we generally use the term. In each context, some sort of Christian Halakha is clearly suggested. The question is, Does anything of this ethical tradition survive in Paul's extant letters?

Beyond reasonable doubt it survives, in part at least, in the hortatory sections of his epistles. (Rom. 12–13; Gal. 5.13 ff., 6.1 ff.; Col. 3.1–4.6; Eph. 4.17 ff.; I Thess. 4.1 ff., 5.1 ff.) An incidental proof that this paraenetic tradition is to be equated with Paul's hortatory material appears in I Thess. 4.2 ff. Here, after reminding them that they had received from him a tradition for their everyday conduct, he proceeds, 'For ye know what charges (or, exhortations) we gave you through the Lord Jesus Christ', and forthwith breaks into palpable *paraenesis* (a warning against fornication).

Now let us glance at the content of the exhortations. As a rule, we find that they consist of such things as these: lists of vices (especially sins of the flesh) to be shunned, and sometimes, correspondingly, of virtues to be cultivated; 'household rules' dictating the relations which should subsist between husbands and wives, masters and servants, etc.; and a mass of maxims inculcating brotherly love, hospitality, humility, and well-doing generally.

There is, then, a good deal of similarity in all the Pauline exhortations. This would not, of itself, be surprising; but when we compare the Pauline exhortations with the exhortations in other early Christian writings (the Pastoral epistles, I Peter, Hebrews 13, I Clement, Hermas, the Didache, etc.), we cannot help remarking how much of this hortatory material is common to them all (household rules, lists of vices, warnings against sexual sins, and maxims enjoining brotherly love, hospitality, humility, well-doing, etc.). We are driven to conclude that the substance of the Pauline paraenetic tradition is not his own creation, but something common and apostolic.

Finally, these hortatory sections in Paul's epistles have little connection with the theoretic foundations of Paul's ethic. Nor do they seem to have immediate relevance to the churches addressed. The only theory which will fit the facts is that Paul, in common with the other apostolic writers, was drawing from a common pool—some sort of paraenetic tradition. But what tradition is this, and whence was it derived?

To answer shortly, the substance of this paraenetic tradition is drawn from the Jewish-Hellenistic popular ethic. It probably came into Christianity *via* Diaspora Judaism, and was suitably Christianized by means of slight changes and additions.

What happened was something like this. The earliest Christians, convinced that Doomsday was near, were not concerned to frame an ethic for a world destined to speedy dissolution, and were in no wise prepared to issue directions for the multifarious problems of everyday Christian conduct. Time passed, the Parousia hope ceased to burn so brightly, the Church settled down from the missionary to the pastoral stage, and Christian teachers were faced with the problem of supplying such directions. They had, to be sure, collections of the words of Jesus, but these did not afford light and leading for all the diverse situations and problems that arose. So they fell back, as we should have expected, on the praxis of Diaspora Judaism. In the course of their proselytizing activities, the Jews of the Diaspora had already amassed a store of ethical rules and precepts (the Jewish document, 'The Two Ways', used by the Didache and Barnabas, shows us how the Christians availed themselves of such Jewish help).

Something of this pre-Christian *paraenesis* can be found, for example, in the apocryphal book of Tobit (written in Egypt, *c.* 200–170 BC).

Tobit summons his son Tobias, and after extracting a promise of burial, proceeds to address a series of exhortations to him.[1] *Inter alia*, he counsels righteousness of life, sexual and marital purity; charity to the poor; brotherly love; honesty in paying wages; sobriety; the Golden Rule; compassion to the hungry and naked; wisdom; fear of the Lord, etc. (4.5–19).

---

[1] Polonius' remarks to his son in *Hamlet* are a good parallel:
'The wind sits in the shoulder of your sail
And you are stayed for. There; my blessing with thee!
And these few precepts in thy memory
See thou character. Give thy thoughts no tongue,' etc.

Since Diaspora Judaism lay open to Greek influences, Hellenism must have contributed its quota to this treasury of *paraenesis*. An example of such Hellenistic hortatory literature is the collection of sayings addressed by the pseudo-Isocrates to Demonicus.

Yet it is not easy to say how far the paraenetic tradition was Jewish, and how far Hellenistic. The maxims of popular ethic and wisdom are often international. We know that the 'lists of vices' are based on Jewish and pagan series (see Deissmann, *Light from the Ancient East*, p. 316, where he cites a popular game of counters in which each counter is marked with the name of a virtue or a vice). Weidinger[1] argues that the 'Household Rules' are of Stoic origin. Such borrowings are altogether likely: do we not find, in Phil. 4.8, Hellenic virtues wrought into a Christian exhortation? 'Just as in the catacombs', says Wand, 'the earliest Christian artists selected such pagan art forms as could be adapted to their purposes, so the early Christian teachers used ethical materials already prepared by the pagan instructors.'[2]

When, therefore, Paul and other Christian missionaries had to give their converts rules and regulations for everyday living, it was from this ready-made store of popular ethic made available by Diaspora Judaism that they naturally drew before proceeding to adapt and Christianize it for their own purposes.

How this was done we can learn from an examination of such 'fixed ground-plans' as the 'Household Rules'. Col. 3.18–4.1 is a good example. The 'rules' here are plainly of 'foreign' origin and have only been faintly Christianized. 'Wives, be in subjection to your husbands as is fitting', but, and here we see the process of Christianization—'in the Lord' (3.18). 'Children, obey your parents in all things, for this is well-pleasing'—again 'in the Lord' (3.20). 'Whatsoever ye do, work heartily'—once more 'as unto the Lord' (3.23). And so forth. Thus social rules of pre-Christian date and origin were enlisted in the service of Christianity.

I have dwelt at some length on the origins of 'the paraenetic tradition'. It remains to emphasize certain aspects of it, as it concerns St Paul.

The fact that 'the word of exhortation' is of general import, and not composed to deal with specific circumstances existing in the

[1] *Die Haustafeln* (1928).   [2] Wand, I Peter (*WC*), p. 5.

church addressed is important for exegesis. Older exegetes were often at pains to explain these admonitions in the light of local conditions. The advice to slaves in Col. 3.22 was probably, so they argued, designed to remove any possible misunderstanding in Colossae resulting from Paul's intervention for Onesimus. The new light shed on the nature of paraenesis should guard us against such interpretations.

The phrase 'the paraenetic tradition' must not be taken to mean that there was a hard-and-fast collection of moral rules—a fixed ethical tradition. A. Seeberg in *Katechismus der Urchristenheit* (1903) conjectured that a catechism of doctrinal and moral directions was at the disposal of the earliest Christian missionaries, and from it were derived Paul's exhortations and 'Household Rules'. But his theory, while rightly emphasizing the formulary elements in the New Testament, did not explain the real *variety* amid similarity in the hortatory passages of Paul and the other apostolic writers. We are concerned, as Dibelius points out, 'not with literary entities but with the occasional problems of missionary praxis', and all that seems demonstrable is that 'we are dealing with traditional material to a certain extent fixed'.[1]

There is, as we have noted, little logical sequence in the succession of precepts which compose the *paraenesis*. They are like assorted beads loosely threaded on the paraenetic string, rather than links in a chain of progressive ethical instruction. On the other hand, a formal connexion is often made by means of link-words, i.e. a word from a preceding sentence is repeated in the following, although there is no inner connexion between the sentences.[2] Thus in Rom. 12.13 ff.:

τοὺς διώκοντας (14*a*) is suggested by τὴν φιλοξενίαν διώκοντες (13)
εὐλογεῖτε (14*b*) is suggested by εὐλογεῖτε (14*a*)
φρόνιμοι (16*c*) is suggested by τὰ ὑψηλὰ φρονοῦντες (16*a*)
μ. πάντων ἀνθρώπων (18) is suggested by ἐνώπιον πάντων ἀνθρώπων (v. 17)

Lastly, Paul and his apostolic compeers were not simply, so to say, purveyors of moral *crambem bis coctam*. Much of their *paraenesis* came from pre-Christian sources; but they had also, in the sayings of Jesus, a new and precious store of moral precepts. (See Chapter V, *supra*, 'The Words of the Lord'.)

[1] I Thess.[3] (*HNT*), p. 20.
[2] We find the same thing in the Gospels: Mark 9.33-7, 41-50.

To sum up: in the hortatory sections of his letters, Paul once again shows his dependence on pre-Pauline Christianity. He borrows from a paraenetic tradition current in the Christianity of his time. That tradition was older than Christianity. But, like many of their modern counterparts, the early preachers of the gospel realized that it was good tactics to take what was best in the pagan ethic of the time, and build on it the structure of their new ethical inheritance in Christ.

VII · St Paul and the Old Testament

EVEN ST PAUL'S USE OF THE OLD TESTAMENT BETRAYS HIS dependence upon the pre-Pauline Christian tradition: he interpreted and used the Jewish scriptures as did his Christian precursors.

This is not to assert that Paul quotes precisely the same Old Testament passages in the same way as those who were Christians before him. What is meant is, first, that he shared the primitive Christian attitude to the Old Testament scriptures and, second, that many of his employments of Old Testament scripture were already 'traditional' in the church before Paul's epistles were written.

The first point need not be laboured. We have already seen (in discussing I Cor. 15.3 ff.)[1] that the first Christians regarded the life, death, and resurrection of Jesus as the fulfilment of the scriptures. In these events, interpreted eschatologically, the Messianic Age had already, in some measure, come to pass. This doctrine of Old Testament scripture peeps out in the pre-Pauline formulae found in I Cor. 15.3 ff. and Rom. 1.3 ff., and in the primitive *kerygma* preserved in Acts. Behind it lies the conviction that Jesus is the promised Messiah to whom 'bear all the prophets witness'.

Paul shared this view. In certain incidental remarks he shows his attitude to Old Testament prophecy and promise very clearly: 'How many soever be the promises of God, in him (Christ) is the yea' (II Cor. 1.20). In I Cor. 10.11 he declares, 'These things (i.e. the Old Testament stories he has been using to warn the Corinthians against idolatry) were written for our admonition, upon whom the ends of the ages are come' (i.e. Christians are living at the terminal points of the two ages—the old and the new).

The second contention—that many of Paul's applications of Old

[1] See Chapter XI, *infra*, on St Paul's eschatology.

58

Testament scripture were 'traditional', in other words, that he used primitive Christian *testimonia*—calls for fuller demonstration. We may accept Rendel Harris's theory that there existed, from the earliest days of the Christian church, some sort of collection of Old Testament proof-texts drawn up to prove the witness of Old Testament scripture to the truth of the Christian faith.

That such *testimonia* were early put together for the use of Christian preachers and apologists in controversy with the Jews, is altogether likely. Similar collections of Old Testament excerpts were probably current in pre-Christian Judaism.[1] How were these earliest Christians to prove to their Jewish opponents that the crucified Galilean whom they worshipped was indeed the Messiah? There was only one effective *argumentum ad hominem* open to them—the elucidation of the Messianic prophecies. Like Apollos at Corinth (Acts 18.28) they had to 'prove by the scriptures that Jesus was the Christ'; to show that the Christians (although they did not as yet possess the name) were the true inheritors of the promises made of old to Israel. Thus the apostles' chief concern was to quote Old Testament passages in vindication of their claims and arguments. 'The fulfilment of prophecy became the main form of Christian evidence. To us, as to the early Gentile hearers, this method would not make so cogent an appeal; and we find it hard to realize the greatness of the need for it amongst Jewish disciples and Jewish antagonists; but that this was the ordinary and natural method of proof is shown by its prevalence throughout the New Testament, and by its persistence even in writings addressed much later to Gentiles, as we see in Justin, Tertullian, Athanasius, and Cyril of Jerusalem.'[2]

Although several scholars before him had suspected the existence of a 'testimony book' which antedated some parts at least of the New Testament, it was Rendel Harris who did the real spade-work and, in two slim volumes,[3] provided us with an adequate proof of the theory.

There is no need here to recapitulate Harris's argument at length, but it will be well to give a brief account of the way in which he

---

[1] See Hatch, *Essays in Biblical Greek*, p. 203.
[2] T. H. Bindley, *The Interpreter*, April 1918, pp. 210–11.
[3] *Testimonies*, Part I (1916) and Part II (1920).

was led to postulate the early existence of such a book of testimonies.

A constant exasperation to the modern student of Patristic literature is the quotation of Old Testament proof-texts to clinch an argument and close a discussion. For example, to quote (with a very significant addition) Psalm 96.10, 'The Lord reigned *from the tree*' as an Old Testament proof of the necessity of Christ's crucifixion seems to us quixotic and absurd. But that kind of argument persisted even down to Athanasius and Nicaea:[1] we find the same sequences of quotations used; the same erroneous ascriptions of authorship (as e.g. in Mark 1.2, 3); the same peculiar translations in independent authors; the same introductory formulae. Justin, Irenaeus, Tertullian, and Athanasius, all show these peculiarities of Old Testament quotation; but the chief happy hunting-ground for them is in two works of a special kind: Cyprian's two books of *Testimonia* addressed to Quirinus, and a collection of Old Testament excerpts attributed to Gregory of Nyssa.

A simple example will suffice. In Irenaeus iv.55, 2, there is a composite quotation from Isa. 35.6, 5; 26.19, and 53.4. In Justin's *First Apology*, 48, we find a similar use of Isa. 35.5.

Irenaeus: [the prophets] who say that '*At his coming* the lame shall leap as an hart, and the tongue of the dumb be plain (verse 6), and the eyes of the blind be opened, and the ears of the deaf hear (verse 5), and the weak hands and feeble knees be strengthened (verse 3), and the dead who are in the tomb shall rise (26.19), and he himself shall bear our weaknesses and carry our sorrows' (53.4), announced these cures which were wrought by him.

Justin: that it was foretold that our Christ should heal all diseases, and raise the dead, hear what was said. It is as follows, '*At his coming* the lame man shall leap as a hart, and the tongue of the dumb shall be plain; the blind shall recover sight, and lepers be cleansed, and the dead shall arise and walk about.'

A full discussion will be found in Harris, *Testimonies*, I, pp. 9–10. Here it is enough to say that the significant addition by both Irenaeus and Justin of the words (not in Isaiah), 'At his coming', plus the displacement in the order of the verses, suggests almost irresistibly that both were using an anthology of testimonies and not independently picking texts from Isaiah.

[1] *Testimonies*, I, pp. 11 f.

Examples might be multiplied. It is clear that such a collection of testimonies was in current use in the second century.[1]

The question is, Did the New Testament writers use such a collection of testimonies, and, in particular, did Paul?

We cannot here consider the problem as it concerns the whole New Testament; it is perhaps enough to say that the erroneous ascriptions of authorship in Mark 1.2, 3 and Matt. 27.9 are best explained by the hypothesis that the evangelists were drawing upon a collection of testimonies.

Did St Paul use such a testimony book? The crucial case is the curious composite quotation in Rom. 9.32 f. The Old Testament original reads:

Isa. 28.16. 'Behold, I lay in Zion for a foundation a stone, a tried stone, a precious corner stone of sure foundation: he that believeth shall not make haste.'

8.14. 'He shall be . . . for a stone of stumbling, and for a rock of offence . . . and many shall stumble thereon.'

Paul writes: 'They stumbled at the stone of stumbling, even as it is written: Behold, I lay in Zion a stone of stumbling, and a rock of offence: and he that believeth on him shall not be put to shame.'

We turn to I Pet. 2.6–8, 'Because it is contained in scripture: Behold I lay in Zion a chief corner-stone, elect, precious: and he that believeth on him shall not be put to shame. For you, therefore, which believe is the preciousness: but for such as disbelieve, the stone which the builders rejected, the same was made the head of the corner; and a stone of stumbling and a rock of offence.'

This is Isa. 28.16 + Ps. 118.22 + Isa. 8.14—without, however, the Pauline dislocation of the passages. Both Paul and Peter differ from the LXX: neither of them, therefore, quotes directly from Isaiah.

Suppose now we turn to Barn. vi.2–4. Here we find Isa. 28.16 (as in Romans and I Peter) set beside Ps. 118.22 (as in I Peter). After noting that Justin (*Dialogue*, c.34) has much to say about the 'stoneship' of Christ, we turn to Cyprian (*Testimonies*, II, 16). The section is headed: *Quod idem et lapis dictus sit*, and there follow Isa. 28.16 and Ps. 118.22. The second passage from Isaiah is not found.

---

[1] A leaf from a fourth-century Testimony Book was recently discovered, and is now in the Rylands Library.

Gregory of Nyssa makes the same references with the same omission, but 'it would take a whole chapter to illustrate the way in which the earliest of the Fathers harp upon the statement that Christ is called the stone in the scriptures'.[1] Nor is it impossible that Christ's own use of the passage from Ps. 118 in Mark 12.10 (and parallels) represents the genesis of the doctrine.

This cannot be 'the long arm of coincidence'. But may it not simply be a case of copying? Peter copied Paul, and later writers followed suit?

If Peter was copying Paul, why did he not copy him more closely? The theory that Peter borrowed here from Romans is bound up with the larger question of the relation between Romans and I Peter. And on this particular problem the trend of recent criticism is quite away from the old view that the parallels between the two epistles prove that Peter borrowed from Paul. Wand,[2] for example, examines the eight passages from Romans in which Sanday and Headlam saw a close parallelism with I Peter. He finds that two are *testimonia* (Rom. 9.25–I Pet. 2.10; Rom. 9.33–I Pet. 2.6, 8); two are common Christian exhortations: a fifth is semi-liturgical; a sixth depends rather on thought than on words; and the remaining two are highly doubtful. I am disposed to agree with Windisch and Wand in denying the alleged dependence. Indeed, it is only on the prior assumption, made by the earlier critics, that Paul originated whatever is common to him and other writers, that the array of parallels between Romans and I Peter is at all impressive. So I accept Harris's view that the most striking parallel of all—this from the 'stone' prophecies—is best explained as due to a common source.

Harris's claims to unearth many other testimonies in Romans are not all equally certain. There are one or two—e.g. Rom. 2.24[3]—to which a query should be affixed. But, in the main, Harris's argument seems to me sound.

It may be objected that, even if I Peter be not dependent on Paul, yet Barnabas, Justin and Irenaeus may so depend. Harris has, I think, rebutted this objection in the case of Justin by showing that,

---

[1] *Testimonies*, I, p. 18.   [2] I Peter (*WC*), p. 19.
[3] Rom. 2.24. 'For the name of God is blasphemed among the Gentiles because of you.' The anti-Judaizing of the Hebrew of Isa. 52.5 by the addition of δι' ὑμᾶς and ἐν τοῖς ἔθνεσιν is claimed (*Testimonies*, II, p. 15) as evidence of Testimony usage. But, as this alteration is made in the LXX, nothing is proved.

apart from the use of testimonies, Justin himself shows hardly any trace of Pauline influence. The same I believe to be true of the epistle of Barnabas, and of Irenaeus.

Of course, if Cyprianic parallels alone were available for many of the alleged testimonies in Paul, we might well be sceptical of the whole theory. The strength of Harris's position lies in his being able to show that in a great assortment of writings—Irenaeus, Justin, Barnabas, and queer odds and ends—we find the same pattern of arguments from Old Testament testimonies where Paul does not come into the picture at all; and further, that in Paul there are unexpressed stages in the argument (see *Testimonies*, II, 19 ff.) which can easily be filled up from this common structure of testimony material.

We only need to get rid of the unproved assumption that Paul is the one reservoir from which flowed all streams of early Christian thought, in order to see the testimony hypothesis as the obvious and natural explanation of the facts. Indeed, second-century Christianity is not Pauline, and there is little reason *a priori* to assume that its controversial materials were borrowed from him.

If these arguments are sound, the importance of Rom. 9.33 is its proof that Paul is not himself culling texts from the Old Testament in order to reinforce his argument, but rather availing himself of a particular application of Old Testament scripture already 'traditional' in the church. This is, of course, by no means an isolated example in Paul's writings. There are others:

Rom. 1.17 (Hab. 2.4). 'The just shall live by faith.'
    4.17 (Gen. 17.5).
    9.25, 26 (Hosea 2.23, 1.10). The doctrine of the Two Peoples.
    10.19, 20 (Deut. 32.21; Isa. 65.1), etc.

There are testimonies also in Galatians, Ephesians, etc. But each alleged *testimonium* must be examined on its own merits.[1]

This is not to suggest that all Paul's citations of the Old Testament came from an anthology of *testimonia*. Paul was too fully saturated in the Old Testament to be wholly dependent on such a

---

[1] The weakness of V. Burch's treatment of Galatians in *Testimonies*, II, is that he depends too largely on Cyprianic parallels.

collection. The words and phrases of the Old Testament had become so much a part of his mental furniture that he could pick and choose quotations to suit his purpose. Nevertheless, there is good reason to believe that many of his scriptural quotations and arguments were traditional in the sense that they had already been employed by his Christian precursors in what was the earliest kind of Christian apologetic.

What follows from all this? First, if, as seems probable, these pre-Pauline *testimonia* existed in some sort of collection or anthology—Harris compares Cromwell's Soldiers' Pocket Bible—we are reminded, as Luke 1.1 explicitly tells us, that there must have existed a good deal of pre-canonical Christian literature.

Second, we have found yet another way in which Paul's debt to his Christian precursors becomes clear. Michel,[1] who is inclined to deny, rather than disprove Harris's whole thesis, complains that the testimony hypothesis impairs Paul's originality. Rather, it accords with all we have been trying to establish. Once again we see how much more there is in Paul's writings that is common and apostolic than the critics have discerned. One example will be enough. It seems likely that what became the famous Lutheran battle-cry, 'The just shall live by faith', was originally a *testimonium*. If that is so, may it not be that the doctrine which we trace back so proudly through Luther to Paul was an item in a pre-Pauline document, and is to be understood, not from Paul alone, but by studying it in its proper place among the *testimonia*?—'The recognition of similar situations is important for the history of doctrine, and it may be that we have been searching in the wrong direction for the gulf which opened between Paul and the Jerusalem pillars.'[2]

---

[1] *Paulus und seine Bibel*, p. 53.   [2] Burch, *Testimonies*, II, p. 32.

VIII · Baptism and the Lord's Supper

SINCE PAUL DID NOT INVENT OR INTRODUCE BAPTISM OR THE Lord's Supper into the Christian church, but took them over, they must be reckoned as part of his inheritance from the pre-Pauline Christian tradition.

So much is clear. But we know little about those rites in the pre-Pauline church, and our scanty data do not enable us to reach many probable conclusions. Let us begin with baptism.

The references in Paul's epistles to baptism are few and difficult to interpret. They are: Rom. 6.3 ff.; I Cor. 1.13–17, 6.11, 10.1–3, 12.13, 15.29; Gal. 3.27; Col. 2.12; Eph. 5.26.

We begin by excluding I Cor. 15.29. This passage is evidence, not for Paul's own view of baptism, but for that of some superstitious Corinthians who had themselves baptized for their deceased friends. Paul neither approves nor condemns the practice. He uses it simply as an *argumentum ad hominem* to demonstrate the illogicality of these Corinthians.

In I Cor. 6.11 and Eph. 5.26, Paul refers indirectly to baptism as a rite of cleansing. Whether he regarded the rite as 'declaratory' or as 'effective', we cannot decide from these passages. Certainly I Cor. 6.11 does not necessarily mean that baptism of itself produces justification and consecration. To affirm that Paul regarded baptism as the *fons et origo* of the new life would be to stultify all that he has to say about faith.

On I Cor. 1.13–17 two observations are pertinent. First, baptism at this time was 'in', or 'into', the name of Christ. Second, no one who regarded baptism as a second principle of salvation on a level with faith would have penned the sentence, 'Christ sent me not to baptize, but to preach the gospel.'

I Cor. 10.1–3 is obscure: in some mystical way the experiences of the Israelites in the wilderness ('the cloud' and 'the sea') are an Old Testament 'type' of Christian baptism.

In I Cor. 12.13 and Gal. 3.27, baptism is the rite of initiation into the Body of Christ. In the first passage, this incorporation into the body is connected with the reception of the Spirit: in the act of baptism, Christians are 'immersed' and 'saturated' in the Spirit as in water. In the second passage (Gal. 3.27), 'As many of you as have been baptized into Christ have put on Christ', the meaning, as Eph. 4.24 shows, is that baptized Christians are 'ensphered' in the corporate Christ, i.e. the corporate community which represents him.

Two passages, Col. 2.12 and Rom. 6.3 ff., remain. Both depict baptism as a burial of the believer with Christ unto death and a resurrection with him into newness of life. The earliest Christian baptism was by immersion, and Christians would not be slow to note the likeness of the actual ceremonial to the fate of their Lord, whose name they publicly professed at baptism. Is Paul's description of the believer dying and rising with Christ in baptism simply an impressive symbol of the moral change which takes place in the believer when, at conversion, he dies to the old pagan life of sin, and rises unto the new Christian life of righteousness?

This is surely to weaken Paul's language. In some sense other than the merely symbolical, Paul conceives the neophyte to become mystically one with his Lord in his death and resurrection. Many find here clear evidence of the infection of Paul's thought by the Greek mystery religions. Schweitzer, on the other hand, would explain the passage in terms of eschatology. But the explanation which seems best to fit the language is in terms of that genuinely Hebrew product, 'prophetic symbolism'.

The prophets of Israel often prefaced, or accompanied, their word with an action (e.g. Jeremiah's breaking of the earthenware flask). Such actions were not merely the oriental love of the concrete. They were more than mere 'action sermons'. On the principle of primitive mimetic magic, they are thought to 'realize' the unseen in the philosophical, as well as the psychological sense. The action is a little part—'a first instalment'—of the reality as yet unseen.

Does not this realistic symbolism adequately explain Paul's language? Rom. 6.1–4 has, as Wheeler Robinson says, a triple aspect: 'it implies the historical events of the death, burial, and resurrection of Christ, of which baptism is the suggestive symbol. It consists of a series of acts on the part of the baptized person who goes down into the water, is submerged, and rises out of it. It supplies a visible parallel to the spiritual experience of the believer, viz. his death to sin and his resurrection to newness of life. All three aspects are implied in the single series of visible acts, and they become sacramental to the participant for whom they have this implication. They constitute something from which the apostle can argue, as from a momentous event. Such significance is warranted in the light of prophetic symbolism, which is much more than mere "representation". There can be no question here of sacramental magic, for the baptized person is a conscious believer, and the efficacy of the rite depends on his conscious and believing participation in it. But, equally, there can be no question of "mere symbolism", for the act is the partial and fragmentary accomplishment of a divine work, the work of the Holy Spirit.'[1] Such an explanation finds a Jewish origin for Paul's language, does justice to the realism of it, and insists that baptism is a real act of God in Christ. In baptism, therefore, the believer is in a partial, but real, sense identified with Christ so that he dies to sin, and rises to new life. All is not done there, but the potency of the new life is implanted in the believer, and his task henceforth is a *Werde das was Du bist*. (Cf. Rom. 6.11.)

For Paul, then, baptism is a rite of cleansing (I Cor. 6.11). It is 'in the name of Christ', i.e. in baptism, that the neophyte passes, once and for all, into Christ's possession. It is the rite of initiation into the corporate Christ (I Cor. 12.13; Gal. 3.27), i.e. the means of admission into the People of God. It is a partial, but real, means of union with Christ in his death and resurrection (Col. 2.12; Rom. 6.3 ff.). The general impression given by Paul's language is that, like most ancients who did not clearly distinguish between the sign and the thing signified, he hesitates between the symbolical and sacramental modes of thought.[2] At all events, faith is the necessary prerequisite of baptism.

---

[1] *The Christian Experience of the Holy Spirit*, pp. 193 f.
[2] Against those who would maintain that baptism of itself in some way produced *ex opere operato* the neophyte's death and resurrection with Christ, it must be said that

But do we know anything of Christian baptism in the pre-Pauline period?

We know little about the beginnings of Christian baptism, and one theory is almost as good as another. In some way, it was connected with John's baptism. (John's significance in the beginnings of Christianity was probably greater than our New Testament writers lead us to believe.)

As far as our meagre evidence goes, the purpose of John's baptism was ethical and spiritual. It was 'a baptism of repentance' (Mark 1.4) designed to ensure 'forgiveness of sins'. Apparently, those who received it regarded it as a sort of passport which would take them safely through the terrors of the impending End into the bliss of the Messianic Age.

That Christian baptism was a mere continuation of John's rite is improbable. The story in Acts 19.1–7 shows that Christian baptism differed from John's in at least two respects: (*a*) on the external side, by the use of the name of Jesus; (*b*) on the spiritual side, by the impartation of the Spirit. The Christian rite of baptism was probably not a continuation of John's rite but a readoption. It must have been introduced very early into the Christian church. Whether Peter's words in Acts 2.38 are historically exact or not, we know that Paul was baptized two or three years later. (To the evidence of Acts 9.18, we can add I Cor. 12.13, where 'we were all baptized', when biographically interpreted, must take us back to about AD 33.) Moreover, these early Christians, in baptizing their converts, must have been conscious that they were acting in accordance with the mind of their Lord. I shall not try to defend the historicity of Matt. 28.18–20 or Mark 16.16; but it can be argued from the very existence and significance of the 'apostolate' that the earliest church leaders must have known of a command from the Risen Lord to evangelize, and that they interpreted this as a command to baptize.[1]

Such baptism was the means of admission into the Messianic community. Its precondition was repentance (Acts 2.38). It was a pledge of identification with the Messiah into whose name (i.e. possession) the neophyte passed. Somehow, whether as concomitant

there are important passages (e.g. Gal. 2.20, 6.14) concerning crucifixion with Christ where baptism does not come into the picture at all.

[1] See Oepke, Kittel's *Th.Wb.* sub βάπτω.

or consequent, the impartation of the Spirit was linked with the rite. So much we may deduce from the references in the early chapters of Acts to baptism.

Can we then say anything about Paul's dependence upon the pre-Pauline Christian tradition in respect of baptism? What elements in Paul's conception are pre-Pauline?

The following suggestions may be hazarded:

Pre-Pauline baptism was 'in', or 'into', the name of Christ. Paul confirms the witness of Acts (Acts 2.38, 8.16, 10.48; cf. I Cor. 1.13 and 6.11). To be baptized into the name of Christ meant to pass into the ownership of Christ. There is no need, in view of such Old Testament passages as Deut. 28.10; Isa. 63.19; and Jer. 14.9 to look anywhere else for the genesis of the 'name' idea than in the Old Testament, although some would argue that the use of the name in baptism has affinities with a pagan superstitious belief in the magical efficacy of a name.

The linkage of baptism with the Spirit is surely pre-Pauline and primitive. 'In one Spirit', says Paul, speaking as though the Spirit were some sort of fluid, 'were we all baptized . . . and were all made to drink of one Spirit' (I Cor. 12.13). 'But ye were washed . . . in the name of the Lord Jesus Christ and in the spirit of our God.' Here the gift of the Spirit is associated with baptism.

In Acts the relation between the two is not so clear. Sometimes baptism apparently precedes the gift of the Spirit (2.38); in Acts 8.14 ff. (conversion of the Samaritans) the sequence is baptism, imposition of apostolic hands, reception of the Spirit (cf. 19.1–7); in Acts 10.44 ff. (Cornelius and his friends) the order is, reception of the Spirit, then baptism. Normally, however (these cases in Acts were probably exceptional), the reception of the Spirit must have synchronized with the act of baptism. Baptism must have been, for the convert, a moment of new power when, with solemn ceremonial, he turned his back on the old life, and began the new. In 'the first, fine rapture', he possibly prophesied or spoke with tongues—he felt an inrush of the Holy Spirit. Moreover, by baptism he became a member of the holy community—the sphere in which the Holy Spirit moved and wrought.

If this be so, we may infer that the linkage of baptism with the reception of the Spirit must have been no peculiar doctrine of Paul's, but an experience felt, in varying degree, by every convert from the first days of the Christian church.

Finally, it is possible that the doctrine of baptism, underlying Rom. 6.3 ff. and Col. 2.12, may not be peculiarly Pauline. Paul introduces it in Romans with the words, 'Surely you know that . . .' (ἢ ἀγνοεῖτε). At the time of writing, Paul had never visited the Roman church: it looked to other founders. If he speaks to Christians, whom he had never seen, of baptism as a sacrament in which the initiate dies with Christ, and rises with him to new life, must we not infer that this doctrine was not peculiar to him, but familiar to Christians generally?[1] Moreover, we recall that in two of Jesus' sayings (Mark 10.38 and Luke 12.50) a martyr death is called a baptism. 'This would hardly be possible if they had not, at that time, looked on baptism as a "dying" and, we might venture to add, as a beginning of a new life. Thus it is not improbable that, already at an early date, baptism was celebrated as a symbol, or as actually a mystical means to a new life: the one baptized emerges from the baptismal water as an entirely new person, the old self no longer exists. Paul developed these ideas further, but it has recently been assumed (by Reitzenstein), and perhaps correctly, that they existed already in the primitive church.'[2]

Was it out of this complex of baptismal ideas that the pre-Pauline hymn of Eph. 5.14 was born?[3]

The Lord's Supper

St Paul did not invent, nor originate, the Lord's Supper. He took it over from the pre-Pauline Christian tradition. So far from being the virtual creator of this sacrament, he has preserved the essential meaning of him who instituted it.

I must now outline the reasons for this conviction. It will be necessary to consider (i) The Last Supper, (ii) The Breaking of Bread in the Primitive Church, (iii) The Pauline Supper.

---

[1] Of course ἢ ἀγνοεῖτε may be only a trait of style (cf. Rom. 7.1).
[2] Weiss, op. cit., pp. 172–3.
[3] Cf. the 'faithful saying' of ii Tim. 2.11:

> 'For if we died with him
> We shall also live with him.'

1 *The Last Supper*

Was the Last Supper Passover or *Kiddush*? We cannot here weigh the pros and cons of either view. Suffice it to say that, despite the arguments of Dalman, Billerbeck, and Jeremias, I think the theory of a Passover *Kiddush* is the best solution of the problem.

We have four accounts of the Last Supper (in Matt. 26, Mark 14, Luke 22, and I Cor. 11). In attempting to get back to the underlying tradition, we begin by excluding the Matthaean account, since it is clearly dependent on the Marcan. The Lucan account presents a serious textual problem. For that reason, and because the 'shorter Western text' possibly depends on Mark,[1] we leave it out of consideration. There remain the Marcan and the Pauline accounts.

Despite important differences, the two accounts are so similar that they must go back to one Aramaic original. It is reasonable to regard what Paul and Mark have in common as derived from that '*Urform*', viz., (*a*) a skeleton framework: Jesus took a loaf, pronounced a blessing, broke it, and said: this is my body. And (he took) a cup, blessed it, and said, this cup is the new covenant in my blood (Paul); [or, this is my blood of the covenant (Mark)]. (*b*) An eschatological utterance (cf. Mark 14.25 with I Cor. 11.26).

What were the actual 'words' over bread and cup? The 'word' over the bread was almost certainly, 'This is my body'. But what was the original form of the word over the cup? Against the Marcan, 'This is my blood of the covenant', two arguments may be levelled: (1) It looks as though the formula has been made to conform to the 'Bread' word by assimilating it to Ex. 24.8. (2) It is hard to conceive Jesus, a Jew, saying to Jews with their horror of blood, 'This is my blood, etc.'[2] For the originality of the Pauline form, we may urge that it not only stands in an older document, but also that it is formally more difficult. However, as Jeremias reminds us, the meaning of both versions is the same.

Now let us consider the meaning of the Supper, beginning with the eschatological utterance.[3] Mark gives it as, 'I will no more drink of the fruit of the vine until the day when I drink it new in the kingdom of God,' i.e., at the heavenly feast in the transcendent

---

[1] Lietzmann, *Messe und Herrenmahl*, p. 215.

[2] Montefiore, *The Synoptic Gospels*, i.332.

[3] Jeremias and Otto believe that Luke, in putting the word at the beginning of the meal, is more original than Mark.

order beyond space and time, since the 'new wine' belongs to the 'new heaven and new earth' of apocalyptic.[1]

How is this utterance related to the 'Words of Institution'? It is often said that they are entirely at variance with each other. But this, as Dibelius has pointed out, is surely wrong. If the action of the Last Supper of itself suggests the founding of a fellowship, the eschatological saying explains why. The two hang together. 'The founding of this table-fellowship in the invisible union with the person of Jesus is necessary because the visible union which hitherto existed is ceasing. Jesus will preside again over this table-fellowship when he can do it in the kingdom of God.'[2]

I Cor. 11.26 confirms this. To the words of institution, Paul joins the remark that the church, by this eating and drinking, 'proclaims the Lord's death *till he come*'. Paul knows of an eschatological *terminus ad quem* for the Eucharist: when the fellowship of the Parousia begins, this memorial table-fellowship will end.

In the eschatological utterance, there lies implicit the command to repeat the rite. Whether Jesus uttered the actual words, 'This do in remembrance of me' or not (and, if we accept the shorter text of Luke 22, Paul is our only authority for them), the idea was clearly in his mind—he desired that the disciples should go on 'doing' it.

Let us turn to the interpretative words over bread and cup: 'This is my body', 'This cup is the new covenant in my blood'. These two words are parabolic words in the manner of him who was a Master of parable.

'This is my body.' The 'is' is the copula of parabolic parallelism[3] (as in Gen. 41.26; Dan. 7.17; Luke 8.11; Gal. 4.24; Rev. 1.20). But what does $\sigma\hat{\omega}\mu\alpha$ mean? The common view that Jesus is here alluding to his body soon to be broken in death, seems unlikely for

[1] Dodd, *Parables of the Kingdom*, p. 56.

[2] Dibelius, *From Tradition to Gospel*, p. 208. 'The connexion between Mark 14.22–4 and 14.25', he writes, 'comes out, as it seems to me, without the least forcing of the text, but is missing indeed if we see in the explanatory words essentially a prophecy of death, and in the prophecy essentially a joyous outlook. Neither can be justified, for the breaking of the bread and the dispensing of the cup are communion rites, and this significance dominates also the accompanying words. And in the prophecy "not again" of the departure comes just as much to expression as the "drinking it new" in the promise of the Kingdom of God.' Further, if Mark 14.25 were only a promise, the wording would be $o\dot{v}$ $\mu\dot{\eta}$ $\pi\acute{\iota}\omega\mu\epsilon\nu$. In limiting the refusal to Jesus, there is the thought that the disciples will drink it again. The reunion is self-explanatory with the outlook upon the Kingdom of God. Matt. 26.29 brings this out expressly in $\mu\epsilon\theta$' $\dot{\upsilon}\mu\hat{\omega}\nu$.

[3] In Aramaic there would be no copula.

two reasons. The 'word' is uttered, not at the actual breaking of the loaf, but as it is being handed to the disciples. And—perhaps more conclusive—there was nothing odd or unusual in the fact that the bread was broken.

Now the Aramaic word underlying σῶμα was probably *guf*.[1] *Guf* means not only 'body' but 'person'. This latter gives excellent sense. 'This is my person—my very self.' In the days to come beyond the Cross, when the disciples repeat the table-fellowship, he will be present with them. The bread is the pledge of his presence in the fellowship. Until their reunion in the Kingdom, their fellowship with their Master shall not cease.

We turn to the 'word' over the cup: 'This cup is the new covenant in my blood.' This cup (the red vintage was gleaming in it) means the new διαθήκη ratified by the death of the Messiah. The words recall Jer. 31.31 f. Jesus by his Messianic work, soon to be crowned by his death, fulfils the prophecy of the new covenant of grace, of which the God-inspired Jeremiah had spoken. And of it, this cup is the effective symbol, effective because the disciples drinking the cup share in the διαθήκη. Like the bread, the cup is pledge and promise of his future presence—the cup a pledge that their Master, soon to die, will be present with them in the fulness of the salvation which his death achieves.

Different the two words are, but their import is the same: 'The promise of the word over the bread is that he will be there; the promise of the word over the cup is that he will be there as the Saviour who establishes the new διαθήκη by his death.'[2] The visible bond between Jesus and his disciples is breaking, but there will be an invisible bond between them. The bread and the cup are the pledges of his presence with them for the time of separation till they meet again.

II *The Breaking of Bread in Acts*

Acts relates that those converted by Peter's preaching at Pentecost 'continued steadfastly in the apostles' teaching and fellowship, in the breaking of bread and the prayers' (2.42). A few verses later,

---

[1] Dalman, *Jesus-Jeshua*, pp. 129 ff.
[2] Behm, to whose article in Kittel's *Th.Wb.* (see sub κλάω) I am deeply indebted in this chapter. It gives a good summary of the results of recent research and outlines a satisfying line of interpretation.

we read: 'Day by day, continuing steadfastly with one accord in the temple, and breaking bread at home (or "from house to house"), they did take their food with gladness and singleness of heart' (2.46). The second half of Acts contains two more references to bread being broken. In Acts 20.7 (the scene is Troas) we read: 'And upon the first day of the week, when we were gathered to break bread, Paul discoursed with them.' Acts 27.35 tells how Paul, at the height of the storm, besought his shipmates to take some food, and when 'he had taken bread, he gave thanks to God in the presence of all: and he brake it, and began to eat'.

What does breaking of bread signify in these passages? Is some sort of Eucharist intended? Not surely in Acts 27, for Paul's shipmates are for the most part pagans, and, moreover, the purpose of the meal is clearly to appease the hunger of famished men. But what of Acts 2.42, 46? Is not this a reference to some sort of Eucharistic meal in the primitive church?

It is usual to equate the Jerusalem church's 'breaking of bread' with the Eucharistic meal of I Cor. 11, i.e. it was a common meal culminating in a reproduction of the Last Supper. This may be correct: in that case the Jerusalem meal is called *a parte potiori*. But since no mention is made of either wine or the death of Christ, Lietzmann would find here the earliest type of Lord's Supper. It was a fellowship-meal beginning with the familiar Jewish rite of the breaking of bread—a continuation indeed of the disciples' table-fellowship with Jesus during his lifetime. The motif of the meal was not the death of Jesus, but the invisible presence of the exalted Lord in their fellowship. The Lord's Supper described in I Cor. 11 was really Paul's creation. He was the first to link the Lord's Supper with the Last Supper. He did so as a result of a special revelation: this, indeed, was what 'he received of the Lord'.

This reconstruction is unconvincing. This is not the meaning of 'I received of the Lord'. Nor is it likely that what, on Lietzmann's view, was an innovation of Paul's, would have been accepted by all the churches, especially the Jewish Christian churches.

But possibly those breakings of bread in the Jerusalem church had nothing at all to do with the Eucharist as we understand the term. The actual phrase, 'To break bread' is thoroughly Jewish. At any meal—a family meal or some more formal occasion—the house-

father was wont, after a thanksgiving, to break the bread and hand it
to those at table. This 'breaking', which was no more than a conventional bit of Jewish ritual, explains many New Testament
passages satisfactorily. Jesus is filling the *rôle* of host when he breaks
the bread by the lakeside, or in the upper room, or at the Emmaus
meal (so also Acts 27). Possibly from this, the opening act of any
Jewish meal, the meals of the Jerusalem church, so briefly described,
take their name. The daily table-fellowship of the primitive church
was not an early type of Lord's Supper; it was simply one of the
forms in which their communal life found expression.

Perhaps the meal at Troas was different. It was held on the first
day of the week, and the language used to describe it recalls some-
what I Cor. 11. (Cf. Acts 20.7, συνηγμένων ἡμῶν κλάσαι ἄρτον
with I Cor. 11.33, συνερχόμενοι εἰς τὸ φαγεῖν = v. 20, συνερχομένων
ἡμῶν κυριακὸν δεῖπνον φαγεῖν. Cf. also Did. xiv.1 and Ign. Eph.
xx.2.)

To sum up: We have no certain evidence in Acts for the pre-
Pauline celebration of the Eucharist. But that such a celebration did
exist, there is no room to doubt. Since Paul in no way claims or
discloses that he was an innovator in the matter of the Lord's
Supper; since it staggers belief that he could have successfully
foisted his innovation (according to Lietzmann's theory) on the
church at large; and since it is difficult to explain the preservation of
the narratives of the Last Supper except on the hypothesis that they
describe the institution of the church's common meal, we may confidently conclude that Christians, from the first, observed the
Eucharist as described in I Cor. 11.

But is it not possible that, in the twenty-odd years intervening
between the original institution and Paul's first visit to Corinth, the
rite had been radically altered in character?

For an answer we turn to Paul.

III *The Pauline Lord's Supper* (I Cor. 10–11)

(1) 11.20–34. The Lord's Supper is a common meal (or *Agapé*)
culminating in the Eucharist. That is the point of 11.20: Paul warns
them that the selfish behaviour of the Corinthian cliques makes impossible any table-fellowship like that of the first Lord's Supper.
For their admonition, he recalls the 'tradition' (which goes back

ultimately to the Lord himself) of the institution of the Supper—a tradition he had delivered to them on his first visit (23–25). The rite is a proclamation of the Lord's death 'till he come' (26). Unworthy partaking—verse 21 shows what 'unworthy' means—of the eucharistic elements is a sin against the body and blood of Christ: to outrage the emblem is to outrage the original (27). Self-examination is essential (28). Failure to discern the thing signified in the sign brings a man under judgment (29). The sick and the dead in Corinth are a sharp proof of divine judgment on them for their profanation of the Lord's Table (30). Self-examination would avoid such judgment. But the present punishment of the Corinthians will deliver them from the doom in store for the world (31–32). For the rest, Christian considerateness should inspire their conduct at the Supper. Mere physical hunger should be satisfied at home. If they so do, they will avoid judgment (33–34).

(2) I Cor. 10.1–5, 14–22. Here, 1–5 is the 'midrash' in which the feeding of the Israelites with manna is a 'type' of the eucharistic bread, and the drinking from the rock of Horeb is a 'type' of the eucharistic cup. The closing remark is significant—'for the rock was Christ'. The following rock (a reference to a rabbinical legend) was the present (pre-existent) Christ.

In 10.14–22, Paul, discussing the problem of eating food sacrificed to idols, touches only incidentally on the Lord's Supper. 'The cup of blessing which we bless, is it not a (means for obtaining) fellowship with the blood of Christ? The bread which we break, is it not a (means for obtaining) fellowship with the body of Christ?' (16). The meaning is that, when Christians bless the eucharistic cup and break the loaf, they are brought into intimate communion, not with themselves only (that is the meaning of verse 17), but with the present Christ. But we see here the beginning of a tendency 'to regard the elements of the meal as a representation of the elements of the person which the concepts "body" and "blood" in the words of Institution recall.'[1]

Verses 20 ff. contrast the cult-meal of the Christians with those of the pagans: in the former the celebrant obtains table-fellowship with the Lord, in the latter with demons. Paul here sets the worship of God and the worship of demons in sharp contrast. The heathen,

[1] Behm, op. cit., p. 739.

he says, sacrifice 'to demons and not to God'. There is for Paul no point of contact between the Lord's Supper and the heathen meals.

So much for Paul's discussion in I Corinthians. Now, we have argued that a Lord's Supper modelled on the Last Supper was current in the Christian church from the first. If the Christians were faithful to their Lord's institution, such a Supper must have had at least three characteristics:

(*a*) It must have been a common meal culminating in a Eucharist.
(*b*) It must have had an eschatological 'forward-look'.
(*c*) Its central significance must have been the presence of Jesus at the table-fellowship of his disciples.

If, as we have reason to believe, Paul's conception of the Lord's Supper owed much to the pre-Pauline Christian tradition,[1] we ought to find in his references to it the characteristics mentioned above.

We find all three.

The Corinthian Lord's Supper was a common meal culminating in a Eucharist.

The eschatological note which Jesus sounded at the Last Supper rings out unmistakably in I Cor. 11.26. The meal stands 'between the times'. It looks backward to the Lord's death; it looks forward to the Parousia.

The central significance of the Lord's Supper was, for Paul, the presence of the Lord with his worshippers. This we deduce from various clues.

The very terms, 'Lord's Supper', 'Lord's Table', imply that at this Supper the unseen Lord is present as host.

In I Cor. 10.1–4, Paul, though speaking of the Old Testament 'sacraments', is clearly thinking in terms of the Christian Eucharist. His underlying thought is: Just as Christ is present at our Christian sacrament, so the pre-existent Christ was present in the Wilderness sacrament.

I Cor. 10.16 points the same way. Paul is warning the Corinthians against participation in pagan sacrificial meals. The pagan meal is 'table' and 'cup' of demons: the Christian meal is 'table' and 'cup' of the Lord. The pagan meal makes the participants κοινωνοὶ τῶν

---

[1] See discussion of I Cor. 11.23 ff. *supra*.

δαιμονίων: the Christian meal makes Christians—the phrase trembles on our lips—κοινωνοὶ τοῦ Χριστοῦ. But Paul does not use the exact phrase. He says that the cup and the loaf mean a fellowship with the 'blood' and 'body' of Christ. It is clear that fellowship with the blood and fellowship with the body mean together fellowship with Christ. Why does Paul not say so? The answer is that the words of institution have influenced his phrasing. In short, the meaning of verse 16 is simply this: You know—all Christians know—that the eucharistic cup and loaf are a means for obtaining fellowship with the unseen but present Christ.

Finally,[1] if *Marana tha* (by itself a prayer for the Parousia), in the context of I Cor. 16.22 and especially Did. x.6, is a eucharistic invocation we have another proof that, for Paul as for the earliest Christians, the presence of Christ was the chief gift of the Supper.[2]

The presence of the Lord with his own in their table-fellowship —that was the intention of Christ in instituting the Supper, and Paul clearly knows it. Nor is I Cor. 11.26 a disproof of this. There, Paul simply alludes to the idea of the new covenant realized by Christ's death with which Jesus himself had interpreted the meaning of his presence at the Supper.

There is much that is dark and difficult in chapters 10 and 11 of I Corinthians; but there is enough to show that Paul reproduces with essential fidelity the institution of the Lord. Could he have done so if he had not been deeply indebted to the pre-Pauline eucharistic tradition?

---

[1] Behm, op. cit., p. 736.

[2] Further confirmation of our point might be found if Anderson Scott is right in translating τοῦτο ποιεῖτε εἰς τὴν ἐμὴν ἀνάμνησιν by 'This do with a view to recalling me' (op. cit., p. 191).

IX · St Paul's Conception of Christ

ST PAUL'S CHRISTOLOGY IS BUILT UPON THE CHRISTOLOGY OF his Christian precursors. The decisive steps in Christology were taken before Paul's time. The primitive church worshipped Jesus as the exalted Messiah and Lord: in that worship lay the germs of all later Christology. Paul, it is true, has drawn out the implications of that earliest Christology, has added new Christological categories, has enriched Christian thinking about Christ by his own personal experience. But the Christ he preaches is the same Christ as his precursors preached. He has simply expounded and interpreted what was implicit in the affirmations of pre-Pauline Christians about Christ.

We might draw this conclusion from the fact that, though Paul clashed with the Jerusalem leaders on other issues, there is no evidence that they ever disagreed on the capital issue of Christology. Paul tells us explicitly (Gal. 2.2) that he submitted the gospel which he preached to the leaders of the Jerusalem church, and gives us no hint that such a central matter as his doctrine of Christ was challenged by them. 'Strange, surely,' says J. S. Stewart, 'that the very point at which critics grow most vociferous in accusing Paul of innovation was one of the few points at which his contemporary critics had no fault at all to find in him.'[1]

It will be the aim of this chapter, not to expound Paul's Christology in all its aspects, but to show that it has its roots in the pre-Pauline conception of Christ. I shall try to show, first, that the chief foundation-stones had been laid in the primitive church—were part of the Christological tradition Paul took over; and, second, that

---

[1] *A Man in Christ*, p. 294. Cf. Jülicher, *Jesus und Paulus* (p. 28), 'We do not hear of any protest against the Pauline picture of Christ from other Christians.'

certain fundamental categories in which Paul thought about Christ were at least pre-Pauline.

At the centre of Paul's conception of Christianity as a religion of salvation stands the person of Christ, its Alpha and its Omega. Everything in the σωτηρία pivots upon the σωτήρ. This Saviour (though Paul uses the title rarely, cf. Eph. 5.23; Phil. 3.20) Paul describes in the most exalted terms. Among the chief honorific titles he applies to him are Messiah, Lord, and Son of God; and in other places he speaks of him as the divine 'Wisdom', the Second Adam, the stone of prophecy, etc. Though he never calls him the Son of Man, this Christological category was, as we shall see, undoubtedly known to him.

Altogether apart from these titles, Paul gives us clear indication of how he conceived of Christ. He asserts his full humanity—'born of a woman', 'made under the law'. But he no less clearly sets Jesus on the divine side of reality. That he actually called him God (cf. Rom. 9.5) is improbable; but he mentions Christ in the same breath with God the Father (Rom. 1.7; I Thess. 1.1; II Cor. 13.14, etc.); calls him God's 'Son' in a sense which we can only describe as unique (Rom. 8.3, 32; Col. 1.13); insists that in him 'dwelleth all the fulness of the Godhead bodily' (Col. 2.9). While he can transfer to Jesus Old Testament language used of Yahweh (Rom. 10.11, 13; I Cor. 1.2, etc.) he conceives of him as subordinate to God (I Cor. 11.3; I Cor. 15.24), and though born and bred as a strict monotheist, he can pray to Jesus *quasi deo*. Further, Paul conceives of Christ as having pre-existed (I Cor. 10.4; Gal. 4.4; Rom. 8.3, etc.), and assigns to him a cosmic *rôle* in creation (I Cor. 8.6; Col. 1.13–18, cf. Eph. 1.10). Finally, Paul links the living Christ with the Spirit, and, while probably not identifying them, can go so far as to say 'The Lord is the Spirit' (II Cor. 3.17).

Such, briefly, is Paul's conception of Christ. It is a very high Christology. The question is, Does it bear any relation to the doctrine of Christ current in the pre-Pauline Christian tradition? Or has Paul transformed his precursors' conception of Christ out of all recognition?

Have we any reliable information how those who were 'in Christ' before Paul conceived of their Master?

The early chapters of Acts purport to give an account of the first

Jerusalem Christians, and of the manner in which they preached Christ. It is generally admitted that Luke is here using early Palestinian traditions which probably existed at first in Aramaic. From the speeches put into Peter's mouth, we learn how Luke thought the earliest Christians attempted to explain the significance of Jesus for faith. Can we place any reliance upon the rudimentary Christology of these speeches? Or do they represent the reading back of later Christological thinking into earlier times?

Let us summarize the Christology of the early chapters of Acts: Jesus is a man of Nazareth approved of God by mighty works (2.22), who after crucifixion and resurrection has been exalted to God's right hand as Lord and Christ (2.33 ff.), and has poured forth the promised Holy Spirit (2.33). In the power of his name, miracles are wrought (3.6, 16). He is the Servant of God (3.13, 26; 4.27)—an allusion to the figure in Deutero-Isaiah—the holy and righteous One (3.14, a Messianic title; Enoch xxxviii.2), the prince of life (3.15, 5.31), i.e. the originator of Messianic salvation, the pre-ordained Christ who will come at the restoration of all things (3.20, 21). He is 'the prophet like unto Moses' (3.22, 7.37)—this is Deut. 18.15 interpreted Messianically—of whose 'days' all the prophets from Samuel have spoken (3.24). He is the stone of prophecy, rejected by the builders, but now made the head of the corner (4.11, quoting Ps. 118.22).

The general impression created by this Christology is that it is thoroughly Jewish and primitive. We may put it this way: if these are not exactly the things that were said about Jesus in the primitive church, they are surely the kind of things that were said. Johannes Weiss,[1] emphasizing its adoptionist flavour, has argued that this Christology is pre-Pauline: 'Whenever and by whomsoever written,' he says, 'it represents a form of Christology which is extremely primitive and certainly pre-Pauline. Peter may actually have used the words:

Now let the whole house of Israel know for a certainty
God hath made him both Lord and Christ,
  This Jesus whom ye crucified' (Acts 2.36).

There is, then, little in this Christology which is historically inconceivable in the primitive church. Details in it have indeed been

---

[1] Weiss, op. cit., I, p. 32.

doubted (Was Jesus called 'Lord' by the earliest Christians? Did the *Urgemeinde* interpret Christ's person and work in terms of Isa. 53?), but the general conception of Christ attributed by Luke to the primitive church does not seem anachronistic.

But, even so, does not a great gulf yawn between this earliest rudimentary attempt to express Christ's significance for faith, and the developed Christology of Paul? Has not the 'Christ-intoxicated' apostle exalted his Master to a position undreamed of by his Christian predecessors?

I propose to argue that it is altogether likely that the primitive church worshipped Jesus as the exalted Messiah and Lord; that this presupposes a cultus (i.e. a properly religious devotion) of Christ; and that, in this confession and cultus of Jesus as the exalted Lord and Christ, lay the essential elements of all later Christology.

It will scarcely be denied that the earliest Christians acknowledged Jesus as the Messiah. (Indeed, it seems impossible to deny that it was as a Messianic claimant that Jesus was put to death, and this means that he must, in his lifetime, have made some claim to be the Messiah.) Now to affirm the Messiahship of Jesus was to affirm a doctrine of his person: it was to assert that Jesus himself, and not merely his teaching, was of vital significance for the people of God. But what did the first Christians mean when they declared Jesus to be the Messiah? It is true that there was not a constant and carefully-defined doctrine of the Messiah in pre-Christian Judaism. Some pictured the coming One as the King Messiah (Old Testament prophecy and the Psalms of Solomon); others thought of the 'Elect One', or supernatural Son of Man (Enoch); other apocalyptic schemes dispensed altogether with the concept of a Messiah. It is suggested that in any attempt to discover what the earliest Christians meant by the Messiahship of Jesus we must choose between these alternatives—'either David's Son or David's Lord, but not both'. I do not think that this atomizing, occidental, twentieth-century criticism (exemplified in *The Beginnings of Christianity*[1]) is sound on this particular score. As far as our evidence goes, it was the claim of Christians from the beginning that Jesus was Messiah, not because he fulfilled this or that particular line of Messianic prophecy, but because he was the fulfilment of the age-long Jewish

[1] Edited by Jackson and Lake.

religious hope as a whole. The burden of the apostolic *kerygma* in Acts is that Jesus, in his life, death, and resurrection, is the fulfilment of all the prophecies (Acts 3.18, 21, 24; 10.43, etc.). The pre-Pauline *paradosis* of I Cor. 15.3 ff. affirms—quite generally—that Jesus' death and resurrection were 'according to the scriptures' (cf. Rom. 1.2 and Rom. 16.26). And Paul shared this common apostolic conviction when he wrote, 'How many soever be the promises of God, in him is the yea' (II Cor. 1.20).

In the primitive church's acknowledgment of Jesus as Messiah, there was involved a doctrine of his person; it was that Jesus as Messiah fulfilled the age-long hope of the people of God.

But there was another equally significant title applied to Jesus by the primitive church. That title was *Maran*, later on Hellenistic soil rendered by κύριος. Bousset, in *Kyrios Christos*, attempted to deny that the primitive church ever worshipped Jesus as Lord. The Christology of the earliest believers was 'a Son of Man dogmatic'. They had no thought of present communion with Jesus. But Bousset never succeeded in explaining away that precious relic of the Aramaic-speaking church's devotion which Paul hurls at his Judaistic opponents in I Cor. 16.23. And criticism since Bousset's time tends to the conclusion that there is nothing historically improbable in representing the primitive church as addressing Jesus as 'Lord'. The verdict of one of the greatest living authorities on this very subject is worth quoting: 'There is no reason for supposing that the word [*Marana tha*] did not originate in the Palestinian mother-church. All the Aramaic words in the gospels come from that source, and the retention of the foreign word is only intelligible if it was derived not from an Aramaic-speaking community in Syria, but from the mother-church itself.'[1]

There can be little doubt that when the primitive church called the *exalted* Jesus *Maran*, they used it in an unmistakably religious sense: it denoted religious veneration; the germ of cultus was in it. ' "Teacher, come!" is an impossible rendering: the phrase can only mean "Our Lord, come!" '[2]

But we can draw another very important conclusion from this precious fragment of Aramaic. It is a prayer—possibly an invocation from the primitive eucharistic service. The earliest Christians,

[1] Foerster in Kittel's *Wörterbuch*, sub κύριος.   [2] Rawlinson, op. cit., p. 235.

monotheists though they were, could pray to their exalted Master. That inference is confirmed by the story of the dying Stephen (Acts 7.59). 'If,' says Lebreton, 'instinctively at the supreme hour of martyrdom, the Christian invokes Jesus, it is because this invocation had become for him a *profound religious habit*.'[1]

The point we are making might be confirmed from the use of the 'name' of Jesus in the primitive church. (Acts 3.6, 16. Cf. Acts 19.13; Matt. 7.22.) Even Bousset in his *Auseinandersetzung* with Wernle admitted that this practice went back to Palestinian Christianity, and presupposed a cultus of Jesus.

All this goes to show that the essential elements of the latter conception of Christ were latent in the earliest church. 'Once the assertion has been made, "Christ is the exalted Lord", the Christology of the primitive church is present in the main features of the doctrine both of his person and his work.'[2] As yet, indeed, there was no systematic attempt to think out what was involved in confessing Jesus as the exalted Messiah, or praying to him as 'Lord', or in invoking his name in healing, exorcism, or baptism. Such reflection came later, and Paul undoubtedly played a notable part in it. But the point to seize is that the data for later Christology are already in existence before Paul comes into the picture at all. There will be development, but no cleavage. If Paul, too, acknowledges Jesus as the exalted Messiah, the complete fulfilment of all God's promises, if he prays to Jesus (as in II Cor. 12.8), if he invokes his name in a peculiarly solemn way,[3] he is simply doing what his precursors did.

Having now tried to establish our first contention, we may go on to the second, namely, that much of Paul's Christology is not the fruit of his own speculation but goes back to pre-Pauline thought about Jesus.

There is no need to dwell further on the titles 'Lord' and 'Christ'. These go back to the primitive church. Suffice it to say that when Christianity moved out into a Hellenistic *milieu*, one title died a natural death, the other took a new lease of life. The title 'Messiah', in its Graecized form, Χριστός, conveyed nothing to the ears of Gentiles who lacked the Jewish background necessary for its under-

---

[1] *Les Origines de Dogma de la Trinité*, p. 329 (quoted by Rawlinson).
[2] Brunner, *The Mediator*, p. 179.
[3] I Cor. 5.4; Col. 3.17; II Thess. 3.6. See Weiss, op. cit., pp. 634 f.

standing. The proof that it was largely unintelligible to Hellenists is seen in their corruption of it into Χρηστός (cf., e.g., Suetonius' well-known reference: *Judaeos impulsore Chresto assidue tumultuantes* (Claud. 25). The same tendency is seen in Paul's letters. Χριστός has ceased, save in a few places (e.g. Rom. 9.5; I Cor. 10.4), to be a title of office, and has become almost a proper name. On the other hand, on Hellenistic soil, the Aramaic *Maran* became ὁ κύριος ἡμῶν —eventually ὁ κύριος—a term perfectly intelligible to Hellenistic people with their 'gods many and lords many'. To a pagan, the word 'Lord' might suggest the idea of the church as a '*thiasos*' of devotees of a cult-deity called Jesus. But for Paul, and the other Christian missionaries with their inheritance of the Septuagint as a safeguard of monotheism, there was no such danger: for them there was 'one God, the Father', and 'one Lord, Jesus Christ' (I Cor. 8.6).

These sentences at once suggest the name of Wilhelm Bousset and his book, *Kyrios Christos*. A brief discussion of his thesis will serve as a good introduction to our second contention.

There was much that was arbitrary and subjective in Bousset's book, and much that later criticism has rejected as wrong; but its abiding merit is that it emphasized the influence and extent of the pre-Pauline Hellenistic Christianity of Antioch and Damascus. Bousset made it clear beyond cavil that the title and cultus of Jesus as Lord, found in Paul, were pre-Pauline.[1] 'It is satisfactory to have it admitted that St Paul did not invent his religion out of his own head; on the contrary, that the presuppositions of his doctrine both of Christ and of the sacraments are to be found in the common faith and practice of the church into which he was baptized, and whose fellowship of life and worship he came to share.'[2] Where Bousset erred was in denying all continuity between the earliest Jewish Christianity and Hellenistic Christianity, and in attributing the alleged transformation of Christianity into a κύριος cult to the influence of the pagan mysteries. Other writers (such as Schweitzer) have dealt faithfully with Bousset's radical error in making Paul, 'the

---

[1] e.g., in various books of the New Testament the Christians are described as 'those who call upon the name of the Lord' (Rom. 10.13; I Cor. 1.2; II Tim. 2.22; I Pet. 1.17; Acts 9.14, 21). This description of the Christians (based on Joel 3.5), was certainly widespread and familiar. Since Paul uses it without explanation, Bousset (op. cit., p. 65) rightly argues that it was not coined (or applied) for the first time by St Paul: it was a pre-Pauline formula.

[2] Rawlinson, op. cit., p. 97.

85

Hebrew of the Hebrews', a Hellenist of the Hellenists. To us it seems that recent criticism, from Weiss's *Urchristentum* down to the researches of the more cautious Form-critics, has largely obliterated the gulf which Bousset set between Paul and the primitive church. 'Essentially all we can discover is a change of emphasis.'[1] For whether the belief in Jesus' Lordship was expressed in the Jewish titles 'Messiah' or 'Son of Man', or in the Hellenistic formulae of Paul and John, makes no decisive difference. In either case the Lord Jesus is 'one who is worshipped, and the Judge at the Final Judgment, on the side of God, essentially over against mankind as a whole'.[2]

We have now to ask, How much more of Paul's doctrine of Christ can we reasonably suppose formed part of the pre-Pauline Christian tradition?

Let us start with the doctrine of pre-existence.

It is tolerably certain that the primitive church called Jesus the Son of Man. Acts represents Stephen as so addressing him, and Mark and 'Q' are evidence that Jesus was so called by the earliest Christians. Now pre-existence was one of the predicates of the apocalyptic Son of Man. In three distinct passages (xlviii.3; xliii.6; lxii.7), the Book of Enoch speaks of the Son of Man as pre-existent. We quote the last one:

> For from the beginning, the Son of Man was hidden,
> And the Most High preserved him in the presence of his might,
> And revealed him to the elect.

If the title Son of Man had been used by Jesus of himself, and had been applied to him by the earliest Christians, it was inevitable that the attribute of pre-existence would soon be added. (It is difficult to think that Peter, and those who had known Jesus in the flesh, were the first to take this step.) But does Paul ever connect the title with Jesus? Indeed, he never applies the rather barbarous Greek phrase, ὁ υἱὸς τοῦ ἀνθρώπου to Jesus, yet there can be little doubt that he thought of Jesus as the Son of Man.[3] The *locus classicus* is I Cor. 15.27 (cf. 15.47). Paul's use here of Ps. 8.6 is only explicable if

[1] K. L. Schmidt, *Die Stellung des Apostles Paulus im Urchristentum*, p. 10.
[2] Brunner, *The Mediator*, p. 179.
[3] See Weiss, op. cit., II, p. 485, and Rawlinson, op. cit., pp. 122 ff. Cf. Heb. 2.6 ff. A 'Son of Man' Christology probably underlies Acts 10.42, 17.31.

Christ be identified with the Son of Man, who is 'made for a short time lower than the angels', that he may be 'crowned with glory and honour'. (Of course originally 'the Son of Man' in Ps. 8 meant 'a mere man'.) In this passage the title Son of Man trembles on Paul's lips. If this be so, we have discovered the source—and it is Jewish, not Greek—of Paul's doctrine of Christ's pre-existence. But since Paul nowhere sets out to establish Christ's pre-existence, but presupposes it as familiar to his readers, and since, as we have seen, it was inevitable, that once Jesus was described as the Son of Man, the predicate of pre-existence would follow, we may confidently conclude that it was no *theologoumenon* of Paul's own, but something axiomatic in the pre-Pauline Christian tradition. And if it should seem strange to us that the early Christians should have predicated pre-existence of One who had so recently lived among men, we should remember that the Jews were wont to postulate pre-existence of objects and men, specially representative of God (Moses, the Temple, the Law, etc.).[1]

Let us take another Christological category used by Paul—what we may call 'the stoneship' of Christ. Twice he alludes to it. In Rom. 9.33 Christ is the stone of stumbling of Old Testament prophecy; in Eph. 2.20 (cf. Acts 3.11) he is the stone, rejected by the builders but now become the head of the corner (Ps. 118.22). As we have seen,[2] it is likely that this 'stone' category was not of Paul's inventing. The coincidence of Old Testament quotation in Rom. 9.33 and I Pet. 2.6–8, is best explained on the hypothesis that both were drawing from a common source, namely, a pre-Pauline collection of testimonies. This collection probably grouped together certain Old Testament texts in order to prove that Christ was the mysterious stone of prophecy. Just such a grouping of texts occurs later in Cyprian with the heading *Quod idem et lapis dictus sit*. To it probably belonged Ps. 118.22 (quoted Acts 4.11 and echoed Eph. 2.20. Cf. Mark 12.10 (and parallels)). In all probability, then, Christians before Paul had seen in Christ the fulfilment of those strange Old Testament verses about the stone.[3]

Let us consider finally the title 'Son of God'. Paul calls Jesus the

---

[1] Cf. Rev. 13.8. 'The Lamb that hath been slain from the foundation of the world.
[2] In the chapter, 'St Paul and the Old Testament'.
[3] Cf. I Cor. 10.4, where Christ is called 'the Rock'. Cf. also Mark 12.10 (and parallels). Perhaps the thought goes back to Jesus himself.

'Son of God' (or 'God's Son', or 'his own Son', or simply 'the Son')
some seventeen times. Was he the first so to describe Christ?
Bousset thought so. The title was a creation of Paul's own. But it
was only by a *tour de force* of German critical legerdemain that he
was able to defend his assertion.[1]

This assertion seems utterly improbable, if only for the reason
that Paul never argues for or defends his ascription of divine sonship to Jesus. No less than seven of his seventeen uses of the title
'Son of God' (or a similar phrase) occur in a letter to a church which
he had not yet visited and which looked to other founders.

But we must examine the matter more carefully. When Paul
describes Christ as the Son of God, he seems to use the title with
two different *nuances*. In some passages he uses it in an official
sense: Son of God is a synonym for Messiah (e.g. Rom. 1.4; I Thess.
1.10; cf. Acts 9.22, with 9.20, where the change in terminology does
not involve any change of meaning). In other passages he thinks of
Jesus as God's Son in a sense which for want of a better word we
can only describe as unique (i.e. in the sense that other men are in
comparison only sons 'by adoption': they are sons as 'found in
him'). Such passages are Rom. 8.3, 32 and Col. 1.13 (where ὁ υἱὸς
τῆς ἀγάπης αὐτοῦ is equivalent to ὁ ἀγαπητὸς υἱός which, following the LXX usage of ἀγαπητός in certain passages, means not
merely 'the dear Son', but 'the only Son').[2]

Now it is altogether probable that Christians before Paul had
called Jesus 'Son of God' in the Messianic sense. The evidence that
'Son of God' was a Messianic title in pre-Christian Judaism is not
abundant. (But cf. 2 (4) Esd. xiii.32, 37, 52; xiv.9.) Still, it is
probable that Ps. 2.7 was explained Messianically in Judaism before
it was explained Christologically in Christianity. And this seems
confirmed by the prominence given to the Psalm in the New Testament. When once Jesus was acclaimed as the Messiah, the alternative title 'Son of God' (= chosen of God) must have lain to hand.
And the stories of the Baptism and Temptation are surely corro-
borative evidence—even if they represent Palestinian *Gemeinde-
theologie*—that the primitive church did so designate Jesus.

But what of the title in its deeper sense? Is it Paul's original
designation of Jesus? This does not seem at all likely. Unless we are

[1] *Kyrios Christos,* pp. 52–7.   [2] Robinson, *Ephesians,* p. 229.

prepared by a kind of critical surgery to remove Mark 12.6; Mark 13.32, and the famous 'Q' saying (Luke 10.21 f. = Matt. 11.25 f.) from the synoptic gospels as church theology of a later date, Jesus did speak of himself as Son in this unique sense. Why should Paul not have learned of this from the church tradition on which, as we have seen time and time again, he was so deeply dependent? It seems far more likely that this doctrine of the unique sonship of Jesus should have come to him as part of the tradition which he received, than that he should have reached it by some superb spiritual intuition of his own.

We must draw our discussion to a close. There are other elements in Paul's conception of Christ which probably go back to the pre-Pauline Christian tradition. In our chapter on the Holy Spirit we suggest that the linkage of the Spirit with the living and exalted Christ which Paul has so fully developed, went back to the primitive church. Anderson Scott thinks it at least possible that Paul's identification of Christ with the divine wisdom which appears most clearly in Col. 1.15–17 may go back to Jesus himself.[1] And so on. Much of all this, of course, falls short of demonstration. But enough has been said to clear St Paul of the charge of being an arch-innovator in the early Christian doctrine of Christ and to show that much of his Christology must be credited not to his own profound spiritual genius but to the pre-Pauline Christian tradition.

Note. It may be asked, Did not the vision on the Damascus road contribute more to Paul's conception of Christ than the Christian tradition? The answer is, Yes and No. The effect of Paul's conversion was not so much to give Paul a new theory about Christ as to convince him of the truth of the claims already made by the Christians. The Crucified, he now realized, was indeed the exalted Messiah and Lord. Stephen and the others had been right.

[1] *Christianity according to St Paul*, p. 264.

X · The Holy Spirit

ST PAUL DID NOT ORIGINATE THE CHRISTIAN BELIEF IN THE
Holy Spirit, which bulks so large in his writings. Behind Paul's rich
doctrine lie the beliefs, experiences, and interpretations of the pre-
Pauline church. The earliest Christians were vividly aware of a new
power invading their life and worship. That power they identified
with God's Spirit bestowed on them by the risen and exalted
Christ, and they interpreted it in the light of Old Testament
prophecy concerning the Messianic outpouring of the divine Spirit
'in the last days'. To these precursors 'in Christ', St Paul was deeply
indebted when he came to formulate his own conception of the
Spirit. What Paul did was not so much to develop the doctrine on
its speculative side, as to draw out the implications of the primitive
church's experience in the light of his own. In effect, he drew the
Spirit and the living Christ closer together; he helped to personalize the Spirit; he ethicized the conception of the Spirit's operation;
and he presented Christianity as the religion of the Spirit.

These statements must now be elucidated.

We must, first of all, try to learn from the early chapters of Acts
what conception of the Spirit prevailed in the primitive church; then
by comparing it with the Pauline conception, try to show how far
Paul took over the beliefs of the earliest believers, and how far he
developed them.

But, right at the start, a problem confronts us. Can we accept the
early chapters of Acts as valid evidence for the beliefs of the first
Christians concerning the Spirit? Have we not here a reading-back
of later ideas into the story of the primitive church? Is not this
picture in Acts, of a Spirit-filled primitive community, simply the
reflection of later conditions when Gentile ideas began to filter into

Christianity? Or—to anticipate another objection—do not the early chapters of Acts betray the all-pervasive influence of Paul? If that is so, all comparison of the doctrine of the Spirit in the early chapters of Acts with the doctrine in Paul's epistles is stultified *ab initio*.

To parry these objections at length is impossible here. I must content myself with stating briefly my reasons for believing that these early chapters in Acts are good evidence for the tone and temper of primitive Christianity.

Paul's doctrine of the Spirit has not coloured the early records in Acts. If the Christology of early Acts is not Pauline, and if the references there to Christ's death do not presuppose Paulinism,[1] there is no *a priori* reason for believing that the conception of the Spirit there presented is the creation of the Apostle to the Gentiles. And even a cursory comparison, say, of Rom. 8 with the allusions to the Spirit in Acts 2, ought to dispel any suspicion that the Pauline doctrine has coloured the early traditions preserved in Acts.

Nor is the other objection more cogent. It is true that contemporary pagan cults were 'enthusiastic' in character. They laid emphasis on ecstasy as a mode of access to divine things. But there is nothing to show that this pagan influence is responsible for the references to the Spirit in Acts.

First, the conception of the Spirit in these chapters is not Gentile but Hebraic. Here is nothing which might not be paralleled from the Old Testament. One example will serve for many. The story of the 'rapture' of Philip the Evangelist (Acts 8.39) strikingly recalls similar language in the Old Testament (I Kings 18.12; II Kings 2.16). 'Whoever is responsible for the basic details of those first chapters of Acts knew exactly what the Old Testament meant by the *ruach adonai*.'[2]

Second, there is no good evidence that belief in the Spirit only emerged when Gentile influence began to permeate Christianity.

Third, the belief in the Spirit is so deeply embedded in New Testament religion that we must suppose it was there from the beginning—and there, let us add, because it was the outcome of real experience. Whatever we make of the story of the Spirit's effusion at Pentecost in Acts 2, only the most sceptical would deny its basal

[1] Cf. Weiss, *History of Primitive Christianity*, vol. I, p. 10.
[2] Snaith, *The Doctrine of the Holy Spirit*, p. 25.

truth—that on a definite occasion the Christian believers in Jeru-salem were convinced they had received a monumental access of new power for the missionary task confronting them.

We turn to the early chapters of Acts with the question: What conception of the Spirit was current in the primitive church at Jerusalem?

To begin with, let us note that we are not dealing with developed theology. The language is that of experimental religion. 'The Spirit' is a term of religious experience, not of systematic theology.

The first main impression we get from these early chapters in Acts is that 'the Spirit' stands for a supernatural, wonder-working power which comes suddenly upon a man. The tendency is to single out abnormal and psycho-physical phenomena as its most charac-teristic manifestations. Glossolalia, the eloquence of Stephen, the shaking of the house, the 'rapture' of Philip, are all ascribed to the illapse of the Spirit of God.

Have these earliest believers any theory about this mysterious power? It is a 'gift' of God (2.38, 8.20, 10.45, etc.). It is mediated by the risen and exalted Christ (2.33). It is the fulfilment of the pro-phecy of Joel (2.16 f.). The sphere in which it operates is the Christian church. Somehow—the evidence is conflicting—it is linked with baptism; whether as precondition or as a consequence.

Is the Spirit conceived of as an influence or as a person? Ancient thinkers loved metaphors and often personified abstractions. We dare not press texts that seem to personify the Spirit. Nor again may we decide that $\pi\nu\epsilon\hat{\upsilon}\mu\alpha$ with the article indicates a 'person', without it an 'influence'. Probably the Spirit was conceived of mostly as an influence, or even *substance* which was 'poured out on men', or with which they were 'filled'. Nevertheless, there are passages which seem to attribute personality to the Spirit (the 'Spirit speaks', 'sends forth', 'hinders', 'testifies'. Men can 'deceive' it, 'tempt' it, 'resist' it).

The concomitants of the Spirit's presence are 'power', 'joy', and 'faith'. With the Spirit ever goes the idea of 'power'. 'Anyone who wants to know the New Testament connotation of Spirit must use his concordance also for the term "power", which is its chief con-tent';[1] that is true of the early chapters in Acts. 'Joy', too, is a

[1] H. W. Robinson, *The Christian Experience of the Holy Spirit*, p. 128.

dominant characteristic of these Spirit-filled men of the primitive church in Acts. The source of the apostle's 'glad fearlessness' (παρρησία) in proclaiming the 'things about Jesus' is the Spirit (4.31). Stephen and Barnabas are depicted alike as men 'full of Holy Spirit and faith' (6.5, 11.24).

We turn to Paul. Does Paul betray any signs that he shared the primitive church's conception of the Spirit, or is his doctrine of the Spirit new, original, *sui generis*—independent of the pre-Pauline Christian tradition?

The answer is, Paul is clearly indebted to pre-Pauline Christianity for much that he has to say about the Spirit. It is true that there are many things in the epistles—Paul's characteristic antithesis of flesh and spirit, his concept of the spiritual body, etc.—which we cannot parallel in our fragmentary records of the primitive church. Yet, in their experience of the Spirit, there are many points of contact between Paul and the earlier Christians.

For example, if I Thessalonians alone of all the Pauline epistles had come down to us, we should have inferred that Paul's conception of the Spirit did not differ at all from that of the primitive church. The epistle has four references to the Spirit. Two of these are anarthrous, as often in Acts (1.5, 6). Like Acts, Paul associates the Spirit with 'power' and 'joy' (1.5 and 1.6). The Spirit is God's gift (I Thess. 4.8), as in Acts. And Paul's exhortation (5.19), 'Quench not the Spirit' (as though he said, Let the flame of the Spirit burn freely), might have been uttered by Peter in his Pentecostal speech. This epistle alone extant, we should never have guessed at the extraordinary richness of Paul's conception of the Spirit.

Let us note some of the ways in which Paul's dependence upon the pre-Pauline Christian tradition concerning the Spirit appears most clearly.

1. Paul reproduces in his own experience the marks of the Spirit as we find them in the early traditions preserved in Acts. Did the earliest believers speak with tongues? Paul himself could 'speak with tongues more than all' (I Cor. 14.18). In the power of the Spirit, he works signs and wonders,[1] including healings. He receives visions, auditions, photisms, and revelations. He, no less than the

[1] Cf. Rom. 15.18 f. 'Things which Christ wrought through me . . . in the power of signs and wonders.'

earliest preachers, has the Spirit's power when he preaches. He, too, knows the same 'joy' and 'boldness' inspired by the Spirit, as the members of the primitive church knew. Like those earliest Christians he has felt the moving of the Spirit as he prayed.[1] In short, Paul has himself experienced the same marvellous and manifold quickening of this strange, new, supernatural power as those 'in Christ' before him, and he speaks of it in the same way.

2. The primitive church and St Paul are at one in their theory of this new power: it is a divine *gift*, and also a 'promised' gift. Peter, at Pentecost, declares that the exalted Jesus, 'having received of the Father the promise ($\epsilon\pi\alpha\gamma\gamma\epsilon\lambda\iota\alpha$) of the Holy Ghost', has 'poured forth this which ye see and hear'; and proceeds to call to repentance and baptism with the promise, 'Ye shall receive the gift ($\delta\omega\rho\epsilon\alpha$) of the Holy Ghost' (Acts 2.38). Paul speaks in the same idiom. The Spirit is God's gift,[2] and that a promised one. 'The promised Holy Spirit', he styles it (Gal. 3.14; Eph. 1.13).

3. Once more, the primitive church and Paul agree in describing the 'symptoms' of the Spirit's presence—notably 'power' and 'joy'.

No one can read these early chapters in Acts without remarking that the dominant characteristic of those who have received the Spirit is $\delta\nu\nu\alpha\mu\iota\varsigma$. In the same way, Paul associates the Spirit with power (Rom. 15.13, 19; I Cor. 2.4; Eph. 3.16).

The Spirit of the primitive church is a Spirit of joy. More than once (as we have already noted) Acts describes the temper of the earliest preaching by $\pi\alpha\rho\rho\eta\sigma\iota\alpha$—a 'glad fearlessness', which astounds the Jewish authorities. The writer of Acts clearly links it with the Spirit—'they were all filled with the Holy Spirit, and began to speak the word $\mu\epsilon\tau\alpha$ $\pi\alpha\rho\rho\eta\sigma\iota\alpha\varsigma$'. And not only does the note of joy ring out in Paul's letters (we think at once of Philippians, 'the epistle radiant with joy'), but he expressly associates this joy with the Spirit. 'God's kingdom', he tells his Roman addressees, 'is not a matter of food-taboos, but righteousness, peace, and *joy* in the Holy Spirit' (Rom. 14.17). 'The harvest of the Spirit is love, *joy*, peace', etc. (Gal. 5.22).

4. The charismata, or 'grace-gifts' of the Spirit described in the early chapters of Acts correspond to those enumerated by Paul. In

---

[1] See Hopwood, *The Religious Experience of the Primitive Church*, p. 194.
[2] Gal. 4.6; Rom. 5.5, 8.15; I Cor. 6.19, 2.12.

I Cor. 12.8–10, Paul provides us with a list of them: wisdom, knowledge, faith, power to heal, power to work miracles, prophecy, the discrimination of spirits, glossolalia, and the interpretation of tongues. The chief charismata in Acts are, of course, speaking with tongues, and prophecy. But Acts and Paul agree in making the Spirit the source of 'healings' and 'miracles'; and in Acts both 'wisdom' and 'knowledge' are associated with the Spirit, if not described definitely as charismata. 'The Seven' are men full of 'the spirit and wisdom' (6.3); Stephen, a man 'full of faith and the Holy Spirit' (6.5).

In all these respects, Paul stands on the same empirical ground as the primitive church. Whatever other influences moulded his thinking about the Spirit, he owed much to the experiences and beliefs of those who were 'in Christ' before him.

Wherein then is St Paul's doctrine of the Spirit original?

First, Paul linked the Spirit with the living Christ as never before. He drew them close together—so close that some have declared that, logically and theologically, he should have been a binitarian.

Yet this was not an entirely Pauline innovation. The earliest believers had associated the gift of the Spirit with the exalted Christ, if not in the same way as Paul. 'Exalted then by God's right hand', Peter's speech at Pentecost runs, 'and receiving from the Father the promise of the Holy Spirit, he (Jesus) hath poured forth this, which ye see and hear' (Acts 2.33).

Paul carries the linkage further. No doubt this is due to his own personal experience, especially his vision on the road to Damascus. 'The Damascus Road experience was identical in content with what other apostles knew as the illapse of the Holy Spirit, but which he felt as the risen and ascended Christ.'[1] At all events, in Paul's epistles, experience of Christ and experience of the Spirit are often indissolubly blended. For Paul, being 'in Christ', and being 'in the Spirit', stand for very much the same thing; and he even goes so far in one passage as to aver 'The Lord is the Spirit' (II Cor. 3.17; cf. I Cor. 15.45).

And yet I do not think Paul in his own mind identified the two. His phrase, 'the Spirit of Christ'[2] (Rom. 8.9), which sets them in

[1] Inge, *Congregational Quarterly*, Oct. 1934, p. 504.   [2] Cf. Acts 14.7.

juxtaposition implies also an effort to differentiate them. Indeed, had Paul been pressed by some twentieth-century occidental theologian with a passion for precise distinctions to make clear his own views, he would, I imagine, have said that the Spirit is the Spirit of God bestowed on believers through the risen Christ.

The consequences of this linking by Paul of the living Christ with the Spirit were vastly important. What Paul really did was to Christianize—or better to 'Christify'—the Spirit.

Paul's second notable contribution (and it really is a corollary of the first) was this: in linking the Spirit with the living Christ, he helped to *personalize* the Spirit. Interpreting the Spirit in terms of the person of Christ, he inevitably ascribed something of the Lord's character and purpose to the Spirit—that is, attributed some sort of personality to what in the primitive church was an influence, energy, or even substance. 'The difference is graphically expressed by the transition from Peter's τοῦτο (this thing) to ἐκεῖνος (that one) in the Fourth Gospel (16.13); and Paul indubitably stands with the latter. This being has character, and character which is known. It is in fact the character of Jesus of Nazareth.'[1]

Once again, Paul seems only to have developed, in the light of his own experience, something that existed in germ in the pre-Pauline church; for certain phrases in Acts concerning the Spirit seem to tremble on the verge of ascribing personality to it.

Yet although Paul did help to personalize the Spirit, it would be straining the evidence to say that he regarded the Spirit as a divine person. The truth would seem to be that Paul's use of certain daring and suggestive phrases (notably in Rom. 8 and in passages like II Cor. 13.14; I Cor. 12.4–6; and Eph. 2.18) set the stage for the long process of Christian thinking that eventually produced the doctrine of the Trinity.

Third: St Paul ethicized the conception of the Spirit's operation.

As the primitive church regarded the Spirit as a wonder-working power, so they saw its manifestations chiefly in phenomena of an abnormal and ecstatic kind—notably glossolalia and prophecy.

Paul saw more clearly. Nowhere is his sanctified common sense more apparent than in his evaluation of spiritual gifts (I Cor. 12–14). He tried to wean his converts from a one-sided association of the

---

[1] C. A. Scott, *Christianity according to St Paul*, p. 144.

Spirit with abnormal and psychophysical phenomena. He insisted that the Spirit was not merely the source of the ecstatic glossolalia which the Corinthians prized so highly, but also a power for worthy living, a dynamic of moral progress. From 'their debauch of religious emotion', he recalled them to the inspiration of duty. He taught them that such everyday, unspectacular virtues as joy, and peace, and love were no less truly the flowering of the indwelling Spirit than 'the tongues of men and of angels'. All spiritual experiences, normal and abnormal, he brought to his Master's test—that of their ethical fruits.

Finally; Paul saw, and set, the whole Christian life within the sphere and control of the Spirit. Or, to put it differently, he made the Holy Spirit the cause 'not only of religious experiences, but of religious experience'.

All Christian life, he tells the Galatians, is lived in the sphere of the Spirit. All Christian graces are its fruit (5.22). The Christian God is he who supplies the Spirit (3.5). To live the Christian life is to walk in the Spirit (5.16). Such teaching was both salutary and necessary. To liberate men, as Paul sought to do, from the discipline of law in religion, without pointing them to some other guide, would have been highly dangerous religious iconoclasm. Paul pointed them to the Spirit which could guide and inspire them as they committed themselves in faith to Christ.

XI · Eschatology

THAT ESCHATOLOGY IS WOVEN INTO THE WARP AND WOOF OF primitive Christianity needs no demonstration at this time of day. Only an illegitimate use of the critical knife will excise it. In eschatology the Christian faith was cradled; it is their eschatological setting that gives a special significance to the gospel facts; and no history of the origins of Christianity which ignores eschatology has any claim to be called scientific.

Since in most other matters of belief and practice Paul stood upon the shoulders of his precursors 'in Christ', it is altogether likely that it was also the case in matters eschatological. The problem of this chapter is: how much of Paul's eschatology may be called pre-Pauline? Or, put otherwise, how much of the common, primitive, Christian eschatology reappears in Paul's writings?

Several factors complicate the issue.

There is no single, consistent eschatological scheme running through Paul's writings. Paul's thinking on the Last Things changed, developed, deepened. He grew in eschatological insight as in grace.

Much of the eschatological apparatus of Paul is a legacy from his pre-Christian Pharisaism. That is clearest in his earliest letters. It took the apostle a long time to wean himself from the traditional thought-forms of Jewish apocalyptic.

The difficulty of dating some of the letters—notably Philippians— is a serious handicap in any attempt to trace the development of Paul's eschatological thinking.

Before we go further, it will be well to have before us some sort of synopsis of Paul's eschatology.

In the development of Paul's eschatology, four stages are roughly traceable:[1] I. The Thessalonian Epistles. II. I Corinthians. III. II Corinthians and Romans. IV. Colossians and Ephesians.

[1] This synopsis is largely based on R. H. Charles, *Eschatology*, p. 378.

Two observations are necessary. First, for critical and eschatological reasons, I cannot bracket Philippians with Colossians and Ephesians. Second, the eschatological differences between I and II Thessalonians do not seem to me irreconcilable.

Stage 1. *The Thessalonian Epistles*

These contain three main eschatological motifs: the great Apostasy and the Antichrist; the Parousia and the Last Judgment; the Resurrection and Final Bliss of the Faithful.

(1) *Apostasy and Antichrist*

The Day of the Lord is impending, but it will not come until Evil culminates in a great apostasy, and the appearance of 'the Man of Sin'. Presently there is 'one that restraineth' (= the Roman Empire). When that factor is removed and the crisis of Evil arrives, Christ descending from heaven will slay the Man of Sin 'with the breath of his mouth' (II Thess. 2.3–12).

N.B. The figure of the Man of Sin, another form of the older myth of Antichrist or Beliar, does not reappear in the later epistles. The mad Caligula may have inspired this portrait of Antichrist.

(2) *Parousia and Last Judgment*

The Parousia is clearly to be in Paul's lifetime (I Thess. 2.19, 3.13, 5.23, etc.). It will ensue upon the crisis of Evil and, though preceded by certain signs (II Thess.), yet will come 'as a thief in the night' (I Thess. 5.2). The event itself is painted in typical apocalyptic colours—Christ with attendant angels descending from heaven, the archangel's voice, the sound of the trumpet, etc. (I Thess. 4.16 f.)

The Parousia is also the Day of Judgment.[1] On that Day, Antichrist will be annihilated, and the wicked doomed to 'eternal destruction' (II Thess. 1.8 f.).

(3) *The Resurrection and Final Bliss of the Faithful*

At the Parousia, 'the dead in Christ' (i.e. Christians who have died before the Parousia) will rise first, then the risen and the

---

[1] The Old Testament phrases for the Day of the Lord are applied to the Parousia (I Thess. 5.2, 4; II Thess. 1.10).

surviving Christians together will be gathered to Christ in the air. Thereafter the elect will pass to endless fellowship with Christ in the transcendent kingdom of God (I Thess. 4.15–17).

N.B. Neither a temporary Messianic reign, nor a resurrection of the wicked is mentioned.

Stage II. *I Corinthians*

Here, clearly, Paul's thought is developing, but he has not yet freed himself from the inherited incubus of Pharisaic eschatology.

(1) *Parousia and Last Judgment*

St Paul still expects the Parousia in his lifetime (I Cor. 4.5, 15.51). 'We shall not all sleep', i.e. Christ will return too soon for that; *Marana tha* (16.22). Tribulations, severe but short-lived (7.26–29), will precede it. Immediately on the Parousia follows the Judgment, with Christ as Judge (I Cor. 4.4, 5).

(2) *The Resurrection*

As Adam and Christ are the inclusive representatives of the two humanities, the natural and the redeemed, so man's hope of resurrection depends on his solidarity with Christ, just as his mortality on his solidarity with Adam (15.22). The resurrection of Christ and that of man are inseparably linked together (6.14). Only the righteous are raised—the true inference from Paul's teaching in chapter 15 about the resurrection body.

According to I Cor. 15.51–52, the resurrection takes place at the Parousia. But this does not consist with the preceding (15.34–49) argument, based on the analogy of the seed, that the resurrection begins immediately after the death of the believer. There is an implicit inconsistency here.

(3) *The Final Bliss of the Faithful*

With the resurrection of the righteous dead and the metamorphosis of the living, death is vanquished (15.26, 51–54). But since death is 'the last enemy', the End has come, when Christ resigns to his Father the kingdom he has ruled since his exaltation.

The resurrection of the righteous dead occurs in a moment at the last trump (15.52). There ensues the transformation of the righteous living. Then begins the consummated kingdom of God in a new world. The 'perfect' state (13.10) has come, and the blessed see God face to face (13.12).

N.B. I cannot follow those who find in I Cor. 15.22–27 a resurrection of non-Christians or a temporary Messianic reign.

Stage III. *II Corinthians and Romans*

Here we note two changes. One concerns the time of the resurrection, the other the scope of the kingdom.

(1) *Universality of Christ's Kingdom*

At Stage I, Paul, still in thraldom to his inherited Jewish beliefs, believed that the world's history was going to end in a crisis of evil and the final impenitence of the mass of mankind (II Thess. 1.8 f.). But now, as we see from Rom. 11, the end of history which Paul envisages is the conversion of all mankind. 'All Israel shall be saved', and God will 'have mercy upon all' (Rom. 11.32). 'The salvation of the elect was clear to him from the beginning, but that was not all; somehow God would save every man.'[1]

(2) *Parousia and Judgment*

The Parousia is still regarded as near (Rom. 13.11–12).[2] It is 'the day of our Lord Jesus Christ' (II Cor. 1.14), i.e. Judgment Day. Christ or God is Judge (II Cor. 5.10; Rom. 14.10 and 2.16). All men must appear and give an account (Rom. 14.10–12).

(3) *The Resurrection*

Heretofore Paul put the resurrection at the Parousia (although we noted at Stage II the emergence of a new belief). Now (II Cor. 5.1–8) he makes the resurrection the immediate sequel of death. We receive, he says, our immortal bodies when we depart this life. II Cor. 5.1–8 therefore asserts what I Cor. 15.34–39 implies.

This is not the only development. Paul no longer speaks of the *resurrection* of the righteous at the Parousia, but of their *manifestation* (Rom. 8.19).

[1] Nock, *St Paul*, p. 204. [2] That this is the only allusion in Romans, is significant.

Stage IV. *Colossians and Ephesians*

These are the epistles of 'the Cosmic Christ'. In them Paul depicts Christ not merely as the creative agent of the universe, but also as the end to which it moves (Col. 1.16). All things are to be 'summed up' in Christ (Eph. 1.10). From this high Christology flow two eschatological consequences:

(1) The everlasting duration of Christ's kingdom. In the final consummation Christ is to be 'all in all' (Eph. 1.23; Col. 3.11; cf. I Cor. 15.28). The goal of the universe is now no longer the completed kingdom of God, in which God is 'all in all', in contrast to the mediatorial kingdom of Christ (I Cor. 15.24–28); it is 'the kingdom of Christ and God' (Eph. 5.5).

(2) Christ's redemptive work is extended to all spiritual beings. All are to share in the reconciliation effected in the Cross (cf. Eph. 1.10: Col. 1.19, 20). 'In I Cor. 15.24 ff. the end was victory, now it was to be a new harmony of all men, all spirits, all things.'[1]

Such, broadly, is Paul's eschatology as usually reconstructed. And as far as it goes, no objection can be taken to it.

But, in reality, 'the half has not been told'. Or, rather, one qualification—and that of quite capital importance—must be made; Paul's eschatology is not only 'futurist'; it is also 'realized'.

We may put it this way. For every pious Jew, all the eschatological hopes and ideals worth living for centred in the Messianic Age, the age to come separated, in traditional eschatology, from this present evil age by the Judgment. Now, though Paul, unlike Jesus, makes relatively little use of the phrase 'the kingdom of God' (employing the precise expression or something like it about a dozen times, and generally of the future consummated kingdom; but cf. I Cor. 4.20 and Rom. 14.17), or ζωὴ αἰώνιος (five times in all), he presupposes in every epistle the salvation for which these phrases stand, and presupposes it as the *present possession* of Christians. For Paul, in a real sense, the kingdom of God has come in the life, death, and resurrection of Jesus conceived as an eschatological process. God has 'visited and redeemed his people'. (What Paul calls 'life in Christ', or life 'in the Spirit', is simply the apostle's expression for what the synoptic Jesus calls 'the kingdom of God', and the Johannine Christ, 'eternal life'.)

[1] Nock, *St Paul*, p. 205.

Paul has many ways of expressing this truth—or rather experience. He puts it very clearly in Col. 1.13, where he speaks of the Father who 'rescued us out of the power of darkness and transferred us into the kingdom of the Son of his love'. But he has other expressions for it. 'If any man is in Christ, there is a new creation' (II Cor. 5.17). Or, 'we are being transformed . . . from glory to glory' (II Cor. 3.18). For Paul the new age had moved forward from the far horizon. Christians were already 'tasting the powers of the age to come'. Salvation was a fact of present experience.

If Paul had been asked for proof, his reply might have been something like this: First, 'He that should come' is come. His name is Jesus. In the person of Jesus—in his life, death, and resurrection —all the Messianic dreams have come true, all the prophecies and promises of God are fulfilled. 'How many soever are the promises of God, in him (i.e. Christ) is the yea' (II Cor. 1.20; cf. Rom. 15.8). Second, Paul would have pointed to the presence and power of the Spirit in the church. The new kind of life, the life of the age to come, of which prophet and apocalyptist had dreamed, was now a present reality. It was life in the Spirit, or 'in Christ'. True, the consummation of life was not yet; but the spirit was 'the first-fruits' and the 'earnest'[1] of that fuller inheritance still to come.

But 'realized eschatology' in St Paul is not a matter of a few isolated texts. Is it not this same experience Paul is trying to express when he speaks of justification or adoption?

According to the traditional eschatological scheme, the Judgment was to come at the end of the present evil age and before the blessed age to come. But Paul declares that Christians are already 'justified', i.e. judged and acquitted. 'The very idea of justification implies a judgment which has already taken place. The righteousness of God is already revealed, and it has taken the form, as the prophets had foreseen that it would, of the justification of his people.'

So, too, with 'adoption'. The apocalyptist had predicted that, in the age to come, they would be 'all sons of their God' (Psalms of Solomon xvii. 30). That blessed time has now arrived, says Paul. 'For as many as are led by the Spirit of God, these are sons of God. For ye . . . received the Spirit of adoption whereby we cry Abba,

---

[1] ἀρραβών: 'a sample of goods guaranteed to be of the same kind as the main consignment.' In Modern Greek, the word means an engagement-ring.

Father' (Rom. 8.14–15). The same conviction—the conviction that Christians are, proleptically, enjoying the life of the age to come—underlies his metaphor of heirship, and his words about the love of God. Already the Christian has begun to share in his glorious heritage (Rom. 8.17); already he possesses the love of God (Rom. 5.5), and nothing shall be able to separate him from it (Rom. 8.35–39). In short, the scheme of traditional eschatology is disrupted—the *eschaton*, the final and decisive act of God—has already entered history, and all it has to offer is already available, in Christ, to the heart that trusts him.

Once this point is taken—and it is fundamental—we can never again regard Paul's conception of the Last Things as simply Jewish Messianism *rechauffé*.

Now, there is no reason to believe that all this was a superb intuition or private discovery of the apostle Paul's. All the evidence indicates that what we mean by the doctrine of 'realized eschatology' was something axiomatic and fundamental in the Christian community when Paul entered it. The belief that Christians were already living in the age of fulfilment was primitive.

The eschatology of the Gospels raises many difficult problems. But there can be no doubt that Jesus regarded the kingdom (or sovereignty) of God as in a real sense present in his person and ministry. Further, the main burden of the apostolic *kerygma* was that in the life, death, resurrection, and exaltation of Jesus the Messiah, and in the effusion of the Spirit, the ancient prophecies had been fulfilled and the signs and wonders of the age to come made manifest. 'This is that which hath been spoken by the prophet . . .'; 'all the prophets from Samuel and those that followed told of the days . . .'; 'we bring you good tidings of the promise made unto the fathers, how that God hath fulfilled the same unto our children'—so the apostolic *kerygma*, preserved in Acts, always began before going on to point to the fulfilment in Christ crucified, risen, and exalted, and in the gift of the Spirit. (The speeches quoted here are, to be sure, not verbatim reports of apostolic sermons in the earliest days of the faith; but it is probable that they preserve a genuinely early Jerusalem tradition, a tradition that shows little influence of Paulinism.)

Moreover, this doctrine of fulfilment (if we may so call it) is not confined to the Acts. It is diffused throughout the whole New Testament. It is in I Peter. It is in Hebrews. It is in the Fourth Gospel and the First Epistle of St John. Through the manifold differences of the various New Testament writings runs the golden thread of realized eschatology.

1. If, then, we wish to discover how much of Paul's eschatology may be called pre-Pauline, here is our starting-point. A fundamental element in the eschatology of the pre-Pauline Christian tradition was the grand conviction, based not merely on scripture but on experience, that in the life, death, and resurrection of Jesus, viewed as an eschatological series of events, the New Age had been inaugurated. Rawlinson makes the point when he writes: 'St Paul, when he spoke of the Father as "having delivered" Christians "out of the power of darkness and translated them into the kingdom of the son of his love", was expressing a thought which we have no reason to believe was distinctively Pauline. Already those who had been made partakers of the kingdom of God had experienced the powers of the age to come.'[1]

2. The second main eschatological conviction Paul derived from the pre-Pauline Christian tradition, was the belief in the imminent Parousia of Christ.

Paul probably believed to the end of his days in a speedy return of Christ. The Thessalonian epistles show how strongly Paul held the belief about AD 50; and though we can trace a waning in his conviction of the immediacy of the event—the hope of Parousia is still burning in Philippians (3.20) and Colossians (3.4). If we ask, how did this futurist eschatology centring in the Parousia harmonize in Paul's mind with the conviction that the Messianic Age had already dawned, the answer is, 'The hope of glory yet to come remains as a background of thought, but the foreground is more and more occupied by the contemplation of all the divine riches enjoyed here and now by those who are in Christ Jesus.'[2]

There is no need to produce elaborate proof that the hope of an imminent Parousia was native to Christianity from the beginning. Curiously enough, the early *kerygma* preserved in the speeches of Acts 1–4 makes only one reference to the Second Coming (3.20).

---

[1] *New Testament Doctrine of the Christ*, p. 33.
[2] Dodd, *Apostolic Preaching*, p. 149.

But the fact that there is not a single New Testament writer who does not speak of a speedy Parousia is clear proof how primitive the conviction was. 'Our Lord, come' was the watchword not merely of the church of God in Corinth but of the whole *ecclesia* from Jerusalem to Ephesus (I Cor. 15.22; Rev. 22.20. Cf. Did. x.6; Heb. 10.37, 9.28; II Pet. 3.4, etc.).

Whether this hope of a Second Coming goes back to Jesus himself is perhaps a moot point which cannot be discussed here. That it was part of the earliest church tradition and therefore a belief dominant in the Christian community Paul entered at his conversion, is as certain as any conclusion about primitive Christianity can be.

3. The third element in Paul's eschatology we may confidently ascribe to the pre-Pauline Christian tradition is a belief in a final judgment at the Parousia.

We need not dwell at length on Paul's doctrine of the judgment. The judgment follows immediately on the Parousia. Christ as God's representative (Rom. 2.16) will sit as judge on his tribunal (II Cor. 5.10; I Cor. 4.4–5) and hold the great assize. Sometimes, however, Paul makes God the judge (Rom. 14.10, 3.6; I Cor. 5.13; II Thess. 1.5). Each man's deeds, good or bad, will be tried. Rewards will vary (I Cor. 3.8; II Cor. 9.6), the judgment will concern not only Christians but the world (Rom. 3.6, 1.18 ff., 2.5–12; I Cor. 6.2) and even angels.

The Jewish origin of much of this is plain to see (e.g. in apocalyptic it is sometimes God (Dan. 7.9–12), sometimes the Son of Man (Enoch lxix.27), who is judge). Our concern, however, is not with the pre-Christian antecedents of these ideas, but with the fact of judgment itself as a central doctrine in the earliest Christian preaching. What precisely the earliest preachers proclaimed about the coming judgment, we do not know; but that Paul's Christian precursors proclaimed a day when God would judge the world through Christ is not easily open to doubt. For not only does the apostolic *kerygma* (Acts 10.42) declare, 'This is he who is appointed by God judge of quick and dead', but in the passages where Paul speaks of judgment to come, he appeals to the fact of judgment as something axiomatic, a *datum* of faith (Rom. 2.16; I Cor. 4.5; II Cor. 5.10, etc.); and it is likely that the summary of saving faith taught by catechists to converts contained a declaration on the subject in more or less stereotyped terms.[1]

4. The correlative of Parousia and judgment is resurrection. That the Christian preachers before Paul proclaimed a resurrection of the elect to follow on the Parousia and judgment is altogether probable. But what precise form the preaching of it took, we do not know. Nor is it likely that, say, Peter and Apollos, or James and Paul, held precisely similar views on the mode and scope of the resurrection. Speculation on this score will not take us very far; but it is unlikely that the stricter members of the mother-church in Jerusalem would have ended a reading of I Cor. 15 with a *Nihil obstat*, or uttered a fervent Amen to the 'Larger Hope' of the apostle to the gentiles: 'God hath shut up all unto disobedience, that he might have mercy upon all' (Rom. 11.32).

---

[1] Windisch (I Peter, *HNT*, ad loc.) commenting on the phrase, κρῖναι ζῶντας καὶ νεκρούς (I Pet. 4.5) remarks, 'already a formula'. Cf. Rom. 14.9, ἵνα καὶ νεκρῶν καὶ ζώντων κυριεύσῃ. Acts. 10.42, κριτὴς ζώντων καὶ νεκρῶν; II Tim. 4.1, Χριστοῦ Ἰησοῦ, τοῦ μέλλοντος κρίνειν ζῶντας καὶ νεκρούς Barnabas vii.2, ὁ υἱὸς τοῦ θεοῦ, ὢν κύριος καὶ μέλλων κρίνειν ζῶντας καὶ νεκρούς. 2 Clem. ii.1, περὶ Ἰησοῦ Χριστοῦ . . . ὡς περὶ κριτοῦ ζώντων καὶ νεκρῶν Such phrasing is surely not accidental.

XII · The Sum of the Matter

IN THIS LAST CHAPTER LET US ASSEMBLE THE FRAGMENTS OF pre-Pauline Christianity that we have found, and survey them collectively. To do so will enable us to get a more unified conception of Paul's dependence on the pre-Pauline Christian tradition. Yet we must not expect too much. This investigation has not been exhaustive. We have not laid bare all the pre-Pauline strata in Paulinism. There are others less tractable, less patient of clear identification. We must not expect to be able to bring together a number of pre-Pauline items, and then go on to subtract the sum obtained from what might be called Paulinism, and so accurately divide the Pauline from the pre-Pauline in every detail.

Nevertheless, if our claim to have discovered many evidences of St Paul's dependence on the pre-Pauline Christian tradition be true, then we can, with the results before us, attempt some sort of answer to the question with which we started, How much did Paul take from the common pool of apostolic Christianity existing before, and alongside of himself? Moreover, we are now in a much better position to pass a judgment on the problem of Paul's originality.

First of all, let us succinctly set forth the results:

1. Paul had a much greater knowledge of the historic Jesus—of his life, his teaching, his character—than much doctrinaire criticism has commonly supposed.

While he must have gained some part of this knowledge in his pre-Christian days, much of it must have been mediated to him by the Christian society which he entered after his conversion.

2. There are embedded in the First Epistle to the Corinthians two unmistakable pieces of pre-Pauline Christian *paradosis*. I Cor. 15.3 ff. is the most precious fragment of the pre-Pauline doctrinal

tradition we possess—the oldest 'document' of the Christian church, going back certainly to the first decade after the crucifixion. I Cor. 11.23–25 is a short narrative of the Lord's Supper—probably the form of words used in celebrating the Eucharist in the church of Damascus, whose Christian table-fellowship Paul must have come to know after his conversion.

3. Scattered throughout Paul's epistles are various, more or less identifiable fragments of quasi-credal and kerygmatic formulae. Some of these have been examined in detail. There are probably many more echoes of the primitive apostolic *kerygma* in the epistles.

4. Paul's letters preserve at least two examples of Christian hymns belonging to the pre-Pauline church. Eph. 5.14 is probably an excerpt from a pre-Pauline baptismal hymn sung by the congregation as the neophyte rose from the baptismal wave. Phil. 2.6–11 is a pre-Pauline hymn (with un-Pauline diction and Semitic traits), which celebrates the humiliation and exaltation of Christ the Second Adam, who, conquering the temptation to which the first Adam fell, chose the *rôle* of the Suffering Servant of the Lord (Isa. 53), and was exalted by God to be 'Lord' of the cosmos.

5. Paul, as a member of the Christian society, had access to certain 'Words of the Lord', to three of which he alludes in I Corinthians. Moreover, apart from explicit allusions to sayings of Jesus, Paul clearly had saturated himself in the general tradition of his teaching; for, in the hortatory sections of the epistles, we discovered not only tacit quotations of *logia* of Jesus, but also clear evidence that Paul had leavened his ethical thinking with the great principles enunciated by his Master.

6. Paul and the other apostolic missionaries transmitted a paraenetic, or ethical tradition to their converts. There are several references to such a tradition in Paul's letters; and the substance of that tradition which apparently had only reached a certain stage of fixation, survives in the hortatory sections of his epistles. In origin pre-Christian, that tradition was suitably Christianized (witness the Household Codes) in order to make it usable by Christians.

7. Paul used a collection of Christian *testimonia*, i.e. in his use of the Old Testament he was often a 'traditionalist'. Very early in the history of Christianity—certainly at a pre-Pauline period—there was put together a mass of Messianic proof-texts intended for the use of

Christian apologists in controversy with the Jews. Paul used such a collection.

8. Paul did not invent, or introduce, the rites of Baptism or the Lord's Supper. He found them already existing. There is no evidence that he radically transformed these pre-Pauline rites.

9. Paul's Christology is built upon that of his Christian precursors. In the primitive church's worship of Jesus as exalted Messiah and Lord, lay the essential elements of the later conception of Christ. Paul interpreted, expounded, and enriched what was implied in the earliest Christian affirmations about Christ. He had to interpret Christ's significance for faith in terms intelligible to Hellenists as well as Jews. But the Christ he preached was the same as that preached by his precursors, and there is no evidence that he was ever challenged on the capital issue of Christology.

10. Paul did not create the belief in the Holy Spirit which bulks so large in his writings. Behind Paul's conception of the Spirit lie the experiences and beliefs of the Christian community he entered. In his teaching about the Spirit he is clearly dependent on earlier Christianity.

11. Finally, Paul's eschatology is not all of his own devising, or a legacy from his pre-Christian Pharisaism. Paul's conviction that, in the life, death, resurrection, and exaltation of Jesus, the new age is proleptically present, and the Christians are already tasting the powers 'of the age to come', was also the conviction of those who were 'in Christ' before him. The same is true of his belief in an impending parousia, a last judgment at which Christ shall be judge, and a resurrection of those that are Christ's.

To what conclusions do these results lead us? To begin with, they tell us something of what pre-Pauline Christianity was like. They transport us back into 'the twilight period'. We see how untrue it is to call Paul the founder of Christianity as we know it. The Christian faith did not spring from the teeming brain of a single man of genius. The church and the faith existed before, and alongside of Paul. We can discover something of its beliefs, rites, ethics, experiences. We can, to some extent, know what the pre-Pauline Christians believed; what *kerygma* they proclaimed; what ethical teaching they gave to converts; what sacraments they celebrated, and the kind of hymns they sang; how they conceived of Jesus their

Master, and how they interpreted and used the Old Testament scriptures; how they thought about the Holy Spirit, and what convictions they held about the Last Things.

But our investigation does more than take us back into that 'twilit realm of historical uncertainties'; it raises the whole problem of St Paul's originality; it makes us ask the question, How much of what we call Paulinism is really common and apostolic Christianity?

It is tolerably clear that Paul's creativeness has been exaggerated. Heitmüller put it very well: 'Paul and his churches represent all the evidence we have of Gentile Christianity at this time. Because Paul stands *like an island in the early tradition*, his creativeness and originality probably seem much greater than it really was. We must try to correct our historical perspective. Gentile Christianity existed before Paul and alongside of him. Other Christian missionaries must have accomplished a great deal.'[1] Of Paul, indeed, it may be said,

> Why, man, he doth bestride the narrow world
> Like a Colossus.

Or, at any rate, so it might seem to readers of the New Testament. Thus, it has become a commonplace to say that there is scarcely a book in the New Testament Canon which does not, at some point, betray the all-pervasive influence of Paulinism. We are told that St Mark, the earliest gospel, shows many Pauline traits, and St John, the latest, could not have been written without Paul's work. The epistle of James, so it is averred, shows a reaction against Paul's doctrine of justification by faith; Hebrews is diluted Paulinism with a blending of Alexandrian philosophy; and the author of I Peter borrows directly from the epistle to the Romans.

I should be disposed to question many, if not all, of these statements. Indeed, one future task of scholarship might well be to call in question far more radically this whole hypothesis of the Pauline saturation of the New Testament.

But it is not hard to see why such an erroneous conclusion has been drawn. One chief reason is that the preservation of so large a proportion of Paul's writings has given him an immense and misleading prominence. For this, Marcion must shoulder much of the blame. That Paul's writings occupy about a quarter of the New

[1] *ZNTW*, July 1915, pp. 156 f.

Testament is largely due to him. 'What we really owe to Marcion, I venture to think, is the enormous preponderance of St Paul in our New Testament.'[1] Marcion's canon (a mutilated Luke and ten epistles of Paul) became the basis of the New Testament as we have it today, and thus gave to Paul a prominence which has misled scholars down the centuries.

No wonder Paul seems to 'stand like an island in the early Christian tradition'. But, if there be any truth in our conclusions, this isolation of Paul is a chimera. For—to adapt a quotation—*vixere multi Christiani ante Paulum*. On their labours and writings—if they produced any—oblivion has fallen. Nevertheless, these men played their part in shaping the *kerygma*, and developing the praxis, of the Christian church which Paul joined at his conversion. Our admiration for the work of the great apostle to the gentiles should not make us forget those unknown missionaries of Christ who, in the first two decades of the church's history, spread 'the hallowed fire' from Jerusalem to Antioch, to Damascus, and even to Rome.

But is not this whole line of argument—I mean the assertion of Paul's great and manifold debt to pre-Pauline Christianity—flatly contradicted by Paul himself? Does not Paul protest the complete originality and independence of his gospel? Does he not declare, 'The gospel I preach is not a human affair, no man put it into my hands, no man taught me what it meant, I had it by a revelation of Jesus Christ'? (Gal. 1.11, 12; Moffatt.)

That is plain enough writing, but we can lay too much emphasis on it. These defiant, unqualified assertions are extorted from him in a controversy which is a matter of life or death for him. His apostolic credentials had been aspersed. Stories were circulating that he had been instructed by the apostolic 'college' in Jerusalem. There was not an atom of truth in them! No human factors were at work in his conversion and call to preach the gospel. He is 'an apostle—not appointed by men or commissioned by any man, but by Jesus Christ and God the Father who raised him from the dead' (1.1; Moffatt). So he flashes out these sentences in the heat of passion, and does not stay to qualify them. But utterances like these cannot mean that he owed nothing to the tradition of the church. To have declared that he owed nothing to it would have been to contradict

[1] Burkitt, *The Gospel History*, p. 323.

what he says explicitly in I Cor. 11.23 ff. and I Cor. 15.3 ff. We can believe Paul when he declares that no human intermediaries made him an apostle of Christ—his conversion was 'an arrest' by Jesus Christ—yet, in 'divers portions and in divers manners', he was a debtor to those 'in Christ' before him.

It may be objected by those jealous for the honour of the great apostle that this whole thesis is designed to strip Paul of all his originality, and to suggest that most of Paul's thinking and theology was derivative and second-hand. We think that such a conclusion need not be drawn.

Perhaps an illustration will clarify the point. Let us turn for a moment to Shakespeare. None questions the originality of Shakespeare. Yet does the ascription of supreme originality to Shakespeare mean that he stood alone without debt to the past? On the contrary, he is indebted to the past in every play. His plots he often took from others. Now he recast an old play, now he turned to Plutarch or to Holinshed. Yet, though he borrowed, though in a score of ways he owed a debt to the past, Shakespeare stands out, unapproached and unapproachable, as the most original literary genius in the English language. Why? Is it not Shakespeare who is the new phenomenon? He draws from the past over and over again, but everything he takes is passed through the alembic of his creative mind.

So it is with Paul. In manifold ways he is a debtor to his Christian predecessors. He does not invent the gospel which he preaches: he takes it over—'receives' it. Yet his originality is beyond challenge. What is new is Paul himself—the 'man in Christ'. The substance of the faith he lives by he 'receives', but, in the rich and creative personal experience of the man himself, it becomes a new thing. Will anyone aver that his knowledge of Christ, that supremely intimate mystical union with the living Lord, is second-hand? Sentences like these—'I live, yet not I, but Christ which liveth in me', 'God forbid that I should glory save in the cross of our Lord Jesus Christ, by whom the world is crucified unto me, and I unto the world', 'The life which I now live in the flesh, I live by the faith of the son of God who loved me and gave himself for me', 'For me to live is Christ'—will anyone declare this to be second-hand religion, or doubt that this is the Christian faith, signed and countersigned, by Paul's own experience?

There is much else in Paul's letters besides his own experience of Christ which we can describe, without fear of serious contradiction, as his own—his clear and unshakable conviction of the universality of the gospel, his profound philosophy of history as in Romans, his conception of the spiritual body, elements in his Christology and eschatology, and so on.

Our aim is not to depreciate Paul, but to see his originality in a truer historical perspective. The point we have laboured is that Paul did not live in a vacuum, that he owed much to his precursors, that Paulinism has in it a great deal of common and apostolic Christianity. Too long has there been a great gulf fixed between Paul and earlier Christianity. Too long has a sharp contrast between Paul's Christianity and that of the earliest Christians been regarded as almost an axiom of criticism. That contrast is disappearing. The gap is being closed. Bousset began the work of bridging the gap; but he tried to drive a wedge in between the primitive church and Paul by emphasizing the creative part played by the Christian community at Antioch. But Bousset grossly exaggerated the difference between the faith of the primitive church and that of Antiochene Christianity. All that we can discover is really 'a change of emphasis' and a change of terminology. Development there is, indeed, but there is no cleavage. The substance of the gospel Paul preaches is that of the *Urgemeinde*. 'Whether then it be I, or they, so we preach, and so ye believed' (I Cor. 15.11).

In conclusion, let us summon three witnesses to the truth of our whole contention.

First, J. Weiss:

We underestimate the fact that certain fundamental principles common to all types of Christianity, the faith in the Messiah, the worship of Christ, the sacraments of Baptism and the Lord's Supper, the traditions of the words of Jesus, and information about his life, a whole series of Christian expressions, and likewise the modification, or adaptation, of Jewish and Old Testament points of view and ways of thinking, had been produced by the primitive community and were found already in existence by Paul himself.[1]

Second, James Denney:

[1] Op. cit., p. 2.

Paul's originality is sometimes an affair of dialectic rather than invention. He is original, rather in his demonstration, than his statement of it. The thing about which he thinks and speaks with such independent and creative power, is not his own discovery; it is the common tradition of the Christian faith; that which he delivers to others and on which he expends the resources of his own original and irrepressible mind, he has himself in the first instance received.[1]

Finally, C. H. Dodd:

No doubt his own idiosyncrasy counted for much in his presentation of the gospel; but anyone who would maintain that the primitive gospel was fundamentally different from that . . . found in Paul must bear the burden of proof.[2]

All three are at one in their assertion that Paul's conception of Christianity was essentially the common faith from the first. Paul does not invent the doctrine that 'Christ died for our sins according to the scriptures': he receives it, and pondering it in his own original mind, gives it a new and profound interpretation. Paul does not create the belief in the Holy Spirit: it is an experience of those 'in Christ' before him. But he, having experienced it himself, especially in relation to the risen Christ, strikes out unforgettable phrases to describe its working in the Christian life. Paul is not the first to worship Jesus as the exalted Lord and Christ. Christians in the primitive church did that before him. But he too comes one day, by the grace of God, to worship and adore that same risen and regnant Christ whom once he had persecuted.

That will suffice. If our research has been sound, we have accomplished what we set out to do. We have learned something of the Christianity which existed in 'the twilight period' before our earliest documents, the epistles of St Paul, were written. We have shown that many stones in the great edifice of Paulinism were already quarried and hewn into rough shape before the 'master-builder' took them over. And finally, by emphasizing the 'traditional' elements in St Paul's thinking and theology, we have thrown into bolder relief what is specifically and indefeasibly his own.

[1] *The Death of Christ*, pp. 111–12.   [2] *The Apostolic Preaching*, p. 27.

Appendix · After Twenty Years

WHEN THIS BOOK FIRST APPEARED IN 1940, I FELT, RIGHTLY or wrongly, something of a pioneer. Few had thoroughly explored the pre-Pauline field: it was not widely realized how much Paul owed to his Christian predecessors, and the opinion that he was something of an arch-innovator, or even corrupter, of the Christian faith still commanded the support of many. Unfortunately, because of the outbreak of World War II, the book was 'still-born': it had been printed but not yet published, when the original publishers Nicholson and Watson, went into liquidation. To be sure, the SCM Press effected a partial rescue by buying up what copies of the book they could; but there could be no question of a proper publication at that time when far more important events were happening. I am therefore very grateful for the SCM Press's invitation to revise it in the light of what has been done in the scholarly world of the last two decades. My first thought was to try to revise the whole thing *ab initio*; but after trying my hand on one or two chapters, it became clear to me that the best thing to do was to print the original text (minus misprints) and put my 'second thoughts' in an appendix at the end.

Much work has been done in the pre-Pauline field since 1940. With all of it I cannot of course claim to be familiar, but I will try to set down here the more important advances known to me. In the past two decades new scholars with improved techniques (e.g. skill in detecting Semitisms or catechetical traits in Paul's *paraenesis*) have arisen. When I looked at the original index, I found that Jeremias's name occurred but once and Cullmann's never. How greatly these two *Neutestamentlers* alone have enriched our understanding of 'the twilight period'! But there are many others, like W. D. Davies, who in 1940 had not yet begun their writing on the New Testament. It is an ironical paradox that perhaps nobody (unless it be C. H. Dodd) has done more to emphasize the 'traditional' quality of Paul's Christianity than the man with whose conclusions I find myself most often in disagreement—Rudolf Bultmann. But while disagreeing with him, my gratitude to him abides, for it was he who first suggested to me this line of inquiry.

As will appear, I feel that the work of the last twenty years has materially strengthened my original thesis. But, equally, in the light of later research, my book in places appears 'dated'; new and better arguments for some of my positions have been produced; and in a few matters I have been compelled to change my opinion. How far all this affects my estimate of Paul's debt to his predecessors I will now try to set down as briefly as possible.

I

Pre-Pauline Paradosis

(1) I Cor. 15.3 ff.

If further proof of the pre-Pauline origin of this passage is needed, it will be found in a study of its vocabulary. At least four of the phrases are un-Pauline:

κατὰ τὰς γραφάς is not found elsewhere in Paul.

ὤφθη, 'appeared', occurs only here and in the credal I Tim. 3.16.

οἱ δώδεκα 'the Twelve', has no parallel elsewhere in Paul.

ὑπὲρ τῶν ἁμαρτιῶν ἡμῶν, 'for our sins', is, to say the least, unusual Pauline usage. The apostle generally uses ἁμαρτίαι, 'sins', only in traditional formulae and quotations.[1]

Where did this formula originate? Formerly, I took the view that 'Paul was here reproducing the baptismal creed of the Damascus church—a creed perhaps taught him by Ananias before his baptism'. I should now prefer to think that the tradition stemmed from the Jerusalem church, for the following reasons:

1. Besides the Aramaic form of Peter's name, other evidences in the passage suggest a Semitic original.[2]

---

[1] *Sin* (Bible Key Words), p. 49.
[2] Jeremias, *Eucharistic Words*, p. 130; *The Servant of God*, p. 88.

2. Note Paul's claim (v. 11) that this *kerygma* is identical with that of the Jerusalem church.

3. Since the two apostles named in it, Peter and James (the chief authorities in the Mother Church), were in fact the two Paul met in Jerusalem during his fortnight's visit (Gal. 1.18), 'after three years' (i.e. about AD 35), in order 'to get information from Cephas',[1] they may well be the source of the *paradosis*.

(2) 1 Cor. 11.23-25

My original discussion of this passage needs to be amended in three ways:

(*a*) My argument from the un-Pauline vocabulary of the *pericope* was incomplete. Whereas I found four words or idioms foreign to Paul, Jeremias[2] finds eight. (παραδιδόναι, used absolutely; κλᾶν, without an object; ἐμός, used attributively; ἀνάμνησις; μετά, followed by the infinitive; δειπνεῖν; ὁσάκις; and τὸ σῶμα, used of the body of the man Jesus.)

(*b*) What does 'I received from the Lord' mean? After a six-fold argument against the view that Paul was here appealing to a special divine revelation made to himself, I concluded that I Cor. 11.23-25 was, like I Cor. 15.3 ff., a piece of *paradosis* which, though mediated to Paul by the pre-Pauline church, went back ultimately to the historical Jesus. But, as I now see, Paul means to say more than that Jesus was the first link in a historical chain of tradition. If this had been all he meant, he would hardly have said 'from *the Lord*'.

The true view is Chrysostom's, as revived and expounded by Cullmann.[3] 'From the Lord' points not only to the historical Jesus, but to the *exalted Lord* Jesus as the real author of the Church's tradition. Paul is thinking of the Christ who is present in that he stands behind the tradition and works in it.

I Cor. 7.10 provides an illuminating parallel. 'To the married I give charge (παραγγέλλω: present tense), not I but the Lord, that the wife should not separate from her husband.' It is the exalted Lord who now declares to Christians, through the tradition, what he had taught his disciples about marriage in the 'days of his flesh'.

---

[1] See G. D. Kilpatrick's discussion of ἱστορῆσαι in *New Testament Essays* (*in memoriam* T. W. Manson), pp. 144-9.

[2] Op. cit., p. 131.   [3] *The Early Church*, pp. 60-70.

St Paul conceives of the exalted Christ as the Transmitter behind the apostles.

Proof of the correctness of this view is to be found in those passages where, for Paul, Christ represents a new *Torah*, both in his person and teaching. 'From this', as W. D. Davies[1] puts it, 'is derived his *rôle* as law-giver, i.e. as One who imparts new *halakoth* and gives instructions by the example of his life' (Phil. 2.5).

(*c*) Where did Paul get this piece of liturgical tradition? And how old is it?

These questions raise the further one: How does Paul's account compare with our other primary account in Mark 14.22–25?

The two accounts contain too many verbal differences to lend any colour to the view that they depend on a common Greek source. Nevertheless, so basically like are they in content that they must both derive ultimately from a common Aramaic source. Which account, Mark's or Paul's, has the better claim to preserve it?

In 1940 I was quite unsure of the answer to this question. Having read Jeremias's discussion, I have now little doubt that Mark's is the more primitive version.[2] Mark 14.22–25 bristles with Semitisms—a score in all—surely an impressive proof of its antiquity, even if we may think Jeremias has made the most of his evidence. By contrast, Paul's version has only four. The rest have either been eliminated or given Greek equivalents. Moreover, Paul's version shows a tendency to *clarify*, of which the best example is the addition of the word 'cup' after 'this'. What we have in Paul looks like a Graecizing and clarifying of the tradition in the interests of Gentile converts, among whom presumably this form of words was used.

Where was this church? In Damascus or Antioch? It was in Damascus that Paul was received into the Christian fellowship. Since he was baptized there, there also he may have 'made his first Communion' and heard, for the first time, the words of I Cor. 11.23–25. On the other hand, the traces of remoulding discernible in Paul's *paradosis*, the evidence that it arose in a Hellenistic *milieu*, and the 'longer text' of Luke (which, with Jeremias, Higgins, Preiss,

---

[1] *St Paul and Rabbinic Judaism*, pp. 147 f.

[2] Op. cit., pp. 106–32. V. Taylor, R. H. Fuller and A. J. B. Higgins take the same view.

etc., I take to be original) strongly suggest that I Cor. 11.23–25 preserves the form of words which Paul heard used in the Antioch church when he settled there in the mid-forties of the first century. We cannot be far out if we guess its date to be about AD 40.

II

Pre-Pauline Formulae

In Chapter III I argued that four such formulae were discoverable in Paul's letters: Rom. 1.3–5, 4.24 f., 10.8–9, and the triad 'faith, hope and love'. Subsequent study has confirmed my conclusions on these passages. But there was one passage which, very reluctantly, I excluded from consideration, because I felt I could not argue a strong case. The passage is Rom. 3.24–25 which, literally translated, runs:

24. Being justified for nothing by his grace through the redemption which is in Christ Jesus, 25. whom God set forth as an expiation, through faith, in his own blood, to show his righteousness because of the passing-over of sins previously committed, in the forbearance of God; 26. to show his righteousness in the present time, so that he might be just and the justifier of him who has faith in Jesus.

What is to be said for the view held by several modern scholars that vv. 24–25 contain a pre-Pauline formula?

The syntactical inconcinnity of the opening δικαιούμενοι, the fact that ἱλαστήριον, πάρεσις, and προγίνεσθαι occur nowhere else in Paul, and the concentration of prepositional phrases and genitival constructions (often a mark of liturgical style) may well make us wonder whether 24–25 are Paul's own work. Bultmann[1] is sure they are not. Here (he says) Paul is 'visibly leaning on—perhaps even quoting from—a traditional formula which can perhaps be traced back to the earliest church'. But he believes that Paul inserted two of his own favourite phrases into it—'for nothing, by his grace' (24), and 'through faith' (25).

Here are his three arguments:

1. The description of Christ as ἱλαστήριον occurs nowhere else in Paul.

2. Paul's custom (except where he is following tradition, as e.g.

---

[1] *The Theology of the New Testament*, I, p. 46.

in I Cor. 11.25, 27) is to speak not of 'the blood' of Christ but of 'the cross'.

3. The idea of the Divine δικαιοσύνη demanding expiation for past sins is unparalleled in Paul.

These are good points, but they hardly amount to a conclusive case. Can it be strengthened? Bultmann's pupil, Käsemann,[1] believes it can.

He begins by considering the usual exegesis of Rom. 3.24–26. Exegetes are wont to find a contrast, despite the formal parallelism between 25b (which deals with the past and its sins) and 26a (which deals with the present and its salvation). In the past God over-looked sins; in the present he deals effectively with them. But this exegesis runs into a difficulty: How could Paul describe the past as the time of God's forbearance and indulgence, when he held that it lay under God's wrath? This difficulty disappears if, following Bultmann, we see in 24–25 a Jewish-Christian formula, on which Paul adds his own comment in 26. On this view, both 25 and 26 describe the same saving Act of God, but from two different view-points—one Jewish-Christian, the other Pauline. Paul took over the Jewish-Christian formula of 24–25 (because it was familiar), but in 26 amended it to suit his own theology.

Let me elucidate Käsemann's argument. Bultmann is right, he says, in holding that δικαιοσύνη in v. 25 is an *attribute*, not an activity, of God.[2] Like the Hebrew *chesed*, which δικαιοσύνη sometimes translates in the LXX, it denotes his covenant-faithfulness ('troth'?) and agrees well with the later mention of God's forbearance[3]. On the other hand, in v. 26 'righteousness' bears its usual Pauline meaning —God's vindicating *activity*, God 'setting things right' for his people.

If then we exclude Paul's insertions, the original Jewish-Christian formula must have run something like this:

> Being justified through the redemption which is in Christ Jesus; whom God set forth as an expiation in his blood, to show his righteousness (covenant-fidelity) and forbearance, because of the passing-over of sins previously committed.

---

[1] *ZNTW*, 1950–1, pp. 150–4.

[2] So Denney (*EGT*, ad loc.) who says that righteousness here 'is obviously an attribute on which the sin of the world has cast a shadow'.

[3] See esp. Ex. 34.7 (the renewing of the Covenant) where δικαιοσύνη renders *chesed* in a 'forbearance' context.

In this formula we are moving in the realm of the idea of the old People of God—as in Mark 14.25. The formula views the New Covenant as primarily God's gracious restoration of the old one which had been broken by men's sins. Paul, however, regards the New Covenant as the antithesis of the Old one (II Cor. 3.1–18; Gal. 4.21–31).

Then, in 26, follows Paul's own comment on the formula. 'Yes,' he says, resuming with an almost identical phrase of purpose, 'it was to show his righteousness (saving activity) at the present time, so that he might be just (true to his covenant) and the justifier of him who has faith in Jesus' (i.e. any ungodly pagan. Note Paul's universalism).[1]

In 26 therefore Paul clamps together the two discordant clauses of 25b and 26a, and in the last five words of 26 he strikes the note, so dear to him, of *sola fide*, as he does also by his insertion of 'through faith' in 25.

Such is the argument. Between them, Bultmann and Käsemann have, in my view, made out a credible case for taking 24–25 as a pre-Pauline formula of Jewish-Christian origin.

III

Pre-Pauline Hymns

In 1940 the view that Phil. 2.6–11 was a pre-Pauline hymn (and not a 'purple patch', like I Cor. 13, of Paul's own composing) was certainly a minority opinion. We can hardly call it so any longer. To be sure, men like W. D. Davies,[2] E. Stauffer,[3] L. Cerfaux,[4] and G. B. Caird[5] still remain unconvinced by the four-fold argument drawn from context, style, vocabulary and doctrine, and F. W. Beare[6] thinks that one of Paul's disciples composed the passage. But the theory first propounded by Lohmeyer in 1928 and accepted by Héring in 1937 and by myself in 1940, now claims the support of J. Jeremias,[7] E. Peterson,[8] R. Bultmann,[9] and O. Cullmann.[10] Few

---

[1] There is good reason to believe that Paul was not the first to teach the doctrine of justification by faith. See my *Introducing New Testament Theology*, pp. 108–11; also G. Dix, *Jew and Greek*, p. 45.

[2] *St Paul and Rabbinic Judaism*, p. 42.   [3] *New Testament Theology*, p. 284.
[4] *Christ in the Theology of St Paul*, pp. 374 ff.   [5] *The Apostolic Age*, p. 114.
[6] *Philippians* (1959), p. 78.   [7] *Studia Paulina*, pp. 152 ff.
[8] *Revue Biblique*, LV, 1948, p. 209.
[9] *Theology of the New Testament*, I, pp. 125, 131, 298.
[10] *The Christology of the New Testament*, pp. 174–81.

have gone all the way with Lohmeyer in believing that the Christ Hymn was originally written in Aramaic and sung at the Lord's Supper in the Jerusalem church. But his analysis of the hymn into six stanzas of three lines each seems to most scholars better than Jeremias's division of it into three stanzas of four lines. (In order to carry through his division, Jeremias is compelled to excise not only 'even death on a cross' (8) but also 'in heaven and on earth and under the earth' (10) and 'to the glory of God the Father' (11)—a Procrustean procedure unlikely to commend itself to many.) But Jeremias, rightly in my opinion, takes ἑαυτὸν ἐκένωσεν to be an exact rendering of the Hebrew of Isa. 53.12 (with the reference not to the *Kenosis* of the Incarnation but to the surrender of Christ's life) and makes the point that the Hymn uses the Hebrew Bible, unlike Paul who normally quotes the LXX. The Adam-Christ interpretation of the whole hymn which I adopted in 1940 now claims the powerful support of Cullmann. The fact that Phil. 2.6–11 and Col. 1.15–20 are probably pre-Pauline hymns, plus the fact that Paul presupposes a knowledge of the Adam-Christ contrast among his readers in Rome and Corinth (see Rom. 5.12–21; I Cor. 15.20–28, 45–49; II Cor. 4.4–6) suggest that the Last Adam doctrine was probably pre-Pauline and had a bigger place in the Early Church's thinking than has commonly been supposed.

The reader will find an excellent survey of the whole modern discussion in R. P. Martin's *An Early Christian Confession* (1960).[1]

Commentators (including myself) have been accustomed to find in Col. 1.15–20 a Christological excursus composed by Paul himself in answer to the Colossian heretics. The lofty terms in which the apostle describes Christ form his counterclaim to the derogatory views of the Saviour held by the heretics. These men evidently were ready to accept Christ in a limited way—as a Saviour from sin, perhaps—but they doubted whether he could rescue them from the menace of the spirit-powers in the universe. Hence Paul's bold assertion here of the complete primacy of Christ over all things, whether in creation or redemption.

But at least a dozen modern scholars[2] are not satisfied with this explanation. Only the hypothesis that Paul here makes use of a

---

[1] See also his article on Phil. 2.6 in *Ex. T.*, March, 1959.
[2] They include six German scholars (E. Lohmeyer, R. Bultmann, E. Käsemann, E. Stauffer, C. Maurer, and G. Schille), three French (J. Héring, P. Benoit, and C. Masson) and three American (F. C. Porter, C. R. Bowen and J. M. Robinson).

pre-Pauline (perhaps even a pre-Christian) hymn will, they think, fit all the facts.

To begin with, the style of Col. 1.15-20 differs from normal epistolary style as poetry from prose. It is perhaps more important to note that the section is unrelated to its context both before and after, for it moves far afield from its point of departure in Paul's prayer for the Colossian Christians; while vv. 21 ff. connect back with the deliverance described in vv. 12-14.

Next, we may note the use of the relative pronoun ὅς in vv. 15 and 18. Credal formulae often favour such relative clauses and their thought proceeds by affirmation rather than by argument, as in I Tim. 3.16 now universally admitted to be a fragment of a hymn or creed:

$$ὃς \ ἐφανερώθη \ ἐν \ σαρκί,$$
$$ἐδικαιώθη \ ἐν \ πνεύματι \ κ.τ.λ.$$

The double ὅς in Col. 1.15-20, not obviously natural, even leads us to expect not one but *two* strophes of a hymn.

But does the passage naturally divide up into lines and strophes to form some kind of hymn? Nearly fifty years ago E. Norden,[1] who pioneered research into liturgical style, both Greek and Jewish, found his attention caught by Col. 1.15-20, and the result of closer study was what looked like a hymn consisting of two strophes, each starting with a ὅς.

Let us set down his analysis in an English translation:

Strophe A

15	*Who is* the image of the unseen God, the *first-born* of all creation	A1
16	*For in him were created all things in heaven and on earth*	A2
	Seen and unseen	A3
	Whether Thrones or Dominions	A4
	Or Powers or Rulers	A5
	All things through him and *to him have been created,*	A6
17	*And he himself is* before all things,	A7
	And *all things* in him cohere,	A8
18	*And he himself is* the head of the body, the church	A9

---

[1] *Agnostos Theos*, pp. 250-4. It is fair to add that Norden only claimed to have found in Col. 1.15-20, 'traditional forms of predication', Jewish periods and a Stoic formula.

Strophe B

	Who is the beginning, *the first-born* from the dead,	B1
	That he might become in all things himself pre-eminent	B2
19	For *in him* willed *all* the Fulness to dwell	B3
20	And *through him* to reconcile *all things to him*	B4
	Making peace by the blood of his cross,	B5
	Through him, whether *those on earth*	B6
	Or *those in heaven*	B7

Here, apparently, we have a liturgical unit of two strophes—one, the longer, celebrating Christ's primacy in creation, the other, his primacy in re-creation—in which the impressive correspondences have been italicized. Yet there are also non-correspondences. Moreover, one line, A9, though it corresponds to A7, ought surely, since it belongs to the realm of redemption, to be in Strophe B.

But the correspondences are even more striking, if we isolate these three pairs of lines:

A1 *Who is* the image of the unseen God the *first-born* of all creation

B1 *Who is* the beginning, the *first-born* from the dead.

A2 *For in him* were created *all things* in heaven and on earth

B3 *For in him* willed *all* the Fulness to dwell.

A6 *All things through him* and *to him* have been created.

B4 And *through him* to reconcile *all things to him.*

Not only do the same words recur, they recur in the same order in the two strophes. Shall we put all this down to pure chance? Or shall we say that it betrays the hand of an exacting composer whose hymnodical style—if we may judge from the parallelisms and the early position of the verb—was Semitic rather than Greek? The odds are on the latter explanation.

The question now is: Can we carry the argument for a pre-Pauline hymn a stage further by appeal to the vocabulary and theology of the passage?

Five words are not found elsewhere in Paul: ὁρατά, θρόνοι, κυριότητες, πρωτεύων, and εἰρηνοποιήσας.

Other highly unusual features include:

συνέστηκε: 'cohere'. Not elsewhere in Paul.

ἀποκαταλλάξαι: Cf. Eph. 2.16, but not attested before these letters. Paul's usual word is καταλλάσσειν.

κατοικῆσαι: Cf. Eph. 3.17.

ἀρχή: as a Christological title, not elsewhere in Paul, but cf. Rev. 3.14.

The argument from theological content turns on 'the great Christology' of the passage. It is not disputed that Col. 1.15–20 is a Christological advance on anything else in Paul's commonly accepted letters. Nowhere else does he so boldly give Christ the freedom of the universe. Nowhere else does he say that he is creation's *goal* (cf. Rom. 11.36 and I Cor. 8.6), or declare that the reconciliation wrought through him embraces all beings not only on earth but in heaven. We cannot categorically assert that this view of Christ cannot be Paul's. What we can say is that it is not Paul's in the other letters certainly from his pen.

What conclusion is to be drawn? When we consider the impressive evidence from style and form, remember the *hapax legomena*, and reckon with 'the great Christology', is not the theory which best fits all the facts Bultmann's:[1]

> Col. 1. 15–20 builds on a hymn which was originally in praise of the cosmic rank of Christ.

IV

'Words of the Lord'

Looking back over Chapter V, I find that I missed three or four echoes of Dominical teaching in Paul's letters.

1. In the discussion of Rom. 12–14, to the many examples already given should be added Rom. 12.18, 'If possible, so far as it depends on you, live peaceably (εἰρηνεύοντες) with all men.' Cf. Mark 9.50 and Matt. 5.9.

2. The second passage chosen as a source for *Verba Domini* was I Thess. 4–5. Here what I wrote about I Thess. 5.1 ff., can be strengthened.

Thus, 'For you yourselves know well that the Day of the Lord will come like a thief in the night' (I Thess. 5.2), strongly suggests that Paul and his converts knew Christ's parable of the Burglar (Matt. 24.43 f.; Luke 12.39 f.). 'You know' will then mean: 'You

---

[1] *Theology of the New Testament*, I, p. 178. James M. Robinson, in an article in *JBL*, vol. LXXVI, pp. 270 ff. (to which I am indebted) undertakes to remove Pauline additions to the hymn (e.g. the three phrases about the spirit-powers and 'the church') and to restore misplaced lines to their original positions in the strophes. His attempt is ingenious but, of necessity, rather speculative.

remember the teaching of Jesus I gave you on this point.' Cf. Rev. 3.3 and 16.15.

This is not all. Compare I Thess. 5.3–7 with Luke 21.34–36, and you discover at least five Greek words—mostly of an apocalyptic sort—common to both passages. Paul can hardly be quoting from Luke's Gospel. Yet it looks as if he were familiar with the tradition which underlies Luke 21.34–36.

All this lends colour to the view that sayings of Jesus formed part of the primitive Christian *catechesis*. Evidently the *Verba Domini* of I Thess. 5 were woven into the eschatological part of it.

3. I am now convinced that I Thess. 5.21 quotes an *Agraphon* of Jesus.

St Paul writes:

> Test (δοκιμάζετε) all things:
> Retain the good (τὸ καλὸν κατεχετε)
> And abstain from all bad coinage (εἴδους)

This is too like the *Agraphon* quoted by Clement of Alexandria and many others for it to be pure coincidence:

> Show yourselves tried (δόκιμοι) money-changers:
> Rejecting much,
> But retaining the good (τὸ δὲ καλὸν κατέχουτες)

Jeremias[1] observes that the early Christian writers invariably quote I Thess. 5.21 as a comment on this *Agraphon*, taking εἶδος in the sense of 'sort of money' (Lat. *species*).

4. One more echo of Christ's teaching should be added to my list, Gal. 6.1. When Paul bids the Galatians 'restore the erring brother', he is enunciating the principle laid down in Matt. 18.15 ff., without dwelling on details of procedure. I Cor. 5.4 f., shows that he also knew the further precept about cases where attempted restoration fails.[2]

Adding these fresh examples to the list already given, we find that, altogether, Paul makes express allusion to four or five Words of the Lord, and echoes or silently adapts at least two dozen other teachings of the Lord. Surely this is evidence enough to rebut the charge that he knew next to nothing of the sayings of Jesus, as well

---

[1] *The Unknown Sayings of Jesus*, p. 92.
[2] C. H. Dodd in *Studia Paulina*, pp. 108 f.

as being yet another testimony to Paul's debt to the Christian tradition.

V

The Paraenetic Tradition

Had I been writing Chapter VI today, I would probably have entitled it 'the Catechetical Tradition'. For a new chapter in the study of the 'didactic' portions of the NT epistles began, just after I wrote, with the publication of Philip Carrington's *A Primitive Christian Catechism* (1940). Six years later, in an appendix to his commentary on I Peter, E. G. Selwyn developed Carrington's thesis still further.

It was the argument of my original chapter that there circulated in the early church an ethical as well as a doctrinal tradition; that the substance of this tradition was pre-Pauline (and, in parts, pre-Christian); and that Paul, in using it, depended on the praxis of the pre-Pauline church.

But whereas I trafficked in the generalities of *paraenesis*, Carrington and Selwyn talk more particularly (and with justification) of *catechesis*, i.e. moral instruction for catechumens, and produce abundant evidence for believing that the early Christian missionaries to the Roman Empire, when instructing converts at baptism, used a pattern of *catechesis* which was already, to some extent, fixed. In other words, when in the paraenetic portions of the NT epistles we light on striking similarities in phrase and idea, the explanation is not that one writer was drawing from another (as our scholarly fathers thought) but that Paul, Peter, James and the rest were developing, each in his own way, the common themes of a primitive Christian *catechesis*.

The full evidence for all this must be sought in the books already mentioned. Here only one or two pieces of it can be given.

Consider I Thess. 4.1–9. Here St Paul, recalling an ethical tradition which he had given his readers orally when he founded their church, repeats for their benefit certain 'orders' it had contained:

> 'It is God's will that you be holy'
> 'Abstain from (ἀπέχεσθαι[1]) immorality.'
> 'Show family affection (φιλαδελφία).'
> 'Love one another (ἀγαπᾶν ἀλλήλους).'

---

[1] A rare NT word, but found, significantly, in the Apostolic Decree (Acts 15.20, 29).

Was this *catechesis* something of Paul's own devising? No—for two good reasons: (1) Paul expressly calls it 'tradition'—something he had received; and (2) other apostles imparted much the same *catechesis* to their converts. Turn to I Pet. 1.13–22, 2.11, and you will find Peter laying down very similar moral 'orders':

> 'Be holy in all your conduct.'
> 'Show family affection (φιλαδελφία) and love one
>   another (ἀλλήλους ἀγαπήσατε).'
> 'Abstain from (ἀπέχεσθαι[1]) fleshly lusts.'

This may not seem to carry us very far (though it led Carrington to speak of 'an early Christian Holiness Code'—a sort of Christianized Lev. 17–20—and to refer to the early Church as 'a neo-levitical community'). Therefore let us take a more impressive sample from the evidence. If we compare Col. 3.8–4.12; Eph. 4.22–6.18; I Peter 1.1–4.11; and James 1.1–4.10, we cannot help being arrested by the striking parallelism in the 'headings' and sequence of ideas, thus:

Col.	*Eph.*
Put off (3.8)	Put off (4.22)
The New Man (3.10)	The New Man (4.24)
Be subject (3.18)	Be subject (5.22)
Watch and pray (4.2)	Stand (6.11)
Stand (4.12)	Watch (6.18)

Now compare this with:

I Peter	*James*
The New Birth (1.23)	The New Birth (1.18)
Put off (2.1)	Put off (1.21)
Be subject (2.13)	Be subject (4.7)
Watch and pray (4.7)	. . . .
Resist (5.9)	Resist (4.7)

What this comparative study suggests is not that these apostolic writers were reproducing an existing document but that they were following some more or less accepted form of *catechesis*—in fact, a four-fold pattern with the headings 'Put off (with its corollary "put

[1] See note on previous page.

on")', 'Be subject', 'Watch and pray' and 'Resist' (the devil). In other words, the catechetical tradition they were following enjoined converts to put off pagan sins and put on the new life with all its virtues, to be subject to all proper authorities (wives to husbands, children to parents, slaves to masters, etc.), to be prayerful and vigilant, and to resist the devil and all his works.

Furthermore, notice that in Eph. 4.25; I Pet. 2.1; and James 1.21, the 'Put on' section begins with a 'wherefore' (διό) or a 'therefore' (οὖν), implying that the imperatives of the fourfold pattern depended on some previous doctrinal indicative. And, on investigation, we find that in each case there is a preceding paragraph which describes Christian baptism as a new creation or a new birth.

It looks very much as if the *Sitz im Leben* of this early Christian *catechesis* was baptism, and it may be that the commands 'Put off' and 'Put on' were dramatically symbolized in the baptizand's unclothing before the rite and in his reclothing after it.

Evidence like this suggests we have uncovered authentic traces of a pre-Pauline pattern of baptismal *catechesis* which existed, when Paul was writing, in a relatively fixed form. I have spoken of a four-fold pattern. Probably it was wider in its scope. C. H. Dodd,[1] for example, thinks it contained seven elements: 1. Lay aside pagan vices; 2. Put on 'the new man' (i.e. humanity) with all his virtues; 3. Order your family relations on a proper Christian basis; 4. Respect your leaders or elders; 5. Deal prudently with 'outsiders', i.e. pagans; 6. Be law-abiding citizens and pay your taxes; and 7. In view of the times, be vigilant.

All this means, as Dr G. B. Caird has said,[2] that the Hellenistic Church in Antioch and elsewhere had devised at an early date a sound ethical alternative to the legalism of the Judaists. From their pagan converts the apostolic missioners demanded a high moral standard as the logical issue of that inward change they had undergone at conversion and baptism.

Now let us look at Rom. 6.17. After describing baptism as a dying with Christ and a rising with him into newness of life, and calling on his readers to 'become what they are'—men dead to sin and alive to God in Christ—Paul comments: 'But thanks be to God that,

---

[1] *The Gospel and Law*, pp. 20 f.   [2] *The Apostolic Age*, p. 113.

when you were slaves of sin, you heartily obeyed the pattern of teaching (τύπον διδαχῆς) to which you were committed.' What didactic pattern is this if it is not the *catechesis* we have been discussing—or something very like it?

One final point. If we may speak of a primitive Christian catechism (i.e. some generally accepted pattern of instruction for catechumens) we may also guess, with some probability, at the sources whence its contents were drawn. Jewish catechetical models for proselyte-baptism no doubt provided the missionaries with some guidance.[1] The 'Household Rules' may owe something to Stoic exemplars. Nor must we forget that Gospel motifs and Words of the Lord were also woven into the warp and woof of the catechetical tradition.

VI

St Paul and the Old Testament

The earliest Christians believed that Christ died and rose 'according to the scriptures' (I Cor. 15.3 f.). When they preached, they claimed that the Gospel events fulfilled what the prophets had foretold. Which scriptures had they in mind, and how did they interpret them?

The first edition of this book accepted Rendel Harris's hypothesis of a corpus of primitive Christian *testimonia*. In other words, there was compiled in the earliest days of the Church an anthology of Messianic proof-texts designed to prove the witness of the Old Testament to the truth of the Gospel, and used by missionaries as a kind of *vade mecum* in their discussions with opponents or inquirers. These proof-texts were drawn at random from the Old Testament and isolated from their contexts.

A better solution to the problem of the early Christian use of the Old Testament has now been provided by C. H. Dodd's *According to the Scriptures* (1952). Whereas Harris thought of a collection of isolated proof-texts, Dodd believes that the early Christians chose certain Old Testament sections or *pericopae*—portions from the prophets, certain psalms, etc.—to document and elucidate the main

---

[1] Cf. also the use by Paul, Peter and others, in their catechetical passages, of the imperatival participle (e.g. ὑποτασσόμενοι, 'be subject'). This is not good Greek. Almost certainly it reflects the rabbis' use of the Hebrew participle when framing rules and codes of conduct.

themes of their *kerygma*. These Old Testament sections or blocks were understood as *wholes*; and if we find quotations from them in the New Testament writers, they are pointers to the entire context, not *testimonia* in and for themselves.

Further, when we observe which sections they chose and how they applied them to Christ and the Church, these early Christians appear as men with a consistent method of exegesis based on real insight into the prophetic reading of Israel's chequered story. Thus they drew deeply on certain passages from the prophets and psalms, while apparently neglecting other portions of the Old Testament. And when we study the passages most commonly cited, we find that they have a single 'plot', with three main variations. The first group of passages (Joel 2–3; Zech. 9–14; Dan. 7, 12) deals with the Day of the Lord, and describes God's breaking into history to judge evil, visit and redeem his people, and establish his reign. The second group comprises 'New Israel scriptures' (Hosea, parts of Isaiah, e.g. Isa. 6.1–9.7, 40.1–11, and Jer. 31.10–34). In them we read of God's judgment on Israel and of the emergence of a new and purer Israel or people of God. The third group (Isa. 42.1–44.5, 49.1–13, 50.4–11, 52.13–53.12, plus certain psalms, e.g. 22, 34, 69 and 118), describes the suffering and ultimate victory of God's righteous Servant who is in some way identified with Israel. We spoke of a 'plot' with three variations. In each of these groups of passages God brings Israel through humiliation to glory; and the New Testament shows how the first Christians saw in Jesus and the Church (the new Israel) the fulfilment of all these prophecies.

From this scriptural substructure of the *kerygma* stemmed the basic doctrines of later theologians like Paul, John and the Writer to the Hebrews. In other words, the roots of the developed NT doctrines of Christ, of the Church, and of the Atonement can all be traced back to this pre-Pauline application of the Old Testament scriptures to the Gospel facts.

Such is Dodd's view, and it is now generally acknowledged to be sounder than Harris's hypothesis. Reading Harris, you get the impression that the *testimonia* which the earliest Christians compiled from the Old Testament were little more than sticks with which to rap the knuckles of their controversial opponents. When you read Dodd, you see that the *testimonia* were bigger and more positive things, excerpts from prophets and psalmists which gathered together divinely inspired hopes in old Israel of which Jesus and the Church were the true fulfilment.

How does all this affect Paul's debt to his predecessors? When Paul speaks of Christ as Isaiah's 'stone' (Rom. 9.33, quoting Isa. 28.16 and 8.14) or of his being 'delivered up for our trespasses' (Rom. 4.25, quoting Isa. 53.12), or of his 'sitting at God's right hand' (Rom. 8.34; Col. 3.1, quoting Ps. 110.1) or of the 'hardening' which has befallen Israel (Rom. 11.7; II Cor. 3.14, echoing Isa. 6.9 f.), or of Christians as those who 'invoke the name of the Lord' (Rom. 10.13, quoting Joel 2,32), he was certainly not the first Christian to apply these OT scriptures to Christ. Other NT writers cite, or echo, these passages independently, suggesting that many of these applications were already 'traditional' when Paul wrote.

But this is not all. Suppose we study the use in the New Testament of Ps. 69. One half of v. 9 is quoted in Rom. 15.3, the other half in John 2.17. Was it sheer accident that Paul and 'John', neither knowing each other's work, chose the two halves of a single verse for 'testimony' purposes? Is it not far likelier that both Paul and 'John' were following a tradition in which this whole psalm had already been applied to Christ? And, to confirm this, there are quotations of four other verses from this same psalm in Matthew, Mark, John and Acts.

Now, if we do like research into the Pauline *testimonia* already mentioned, we discover that Dodd's hypothesis survives the test. The early Christians dealt not in single, isolated OT proof-texts chosen at random, regardless of the context, but in whole psalms and continuous sections from the prophets.

Applying the new theory of the early Christian use of the Old Testament to Paul's letters, we can point to at least ten such psalms or prophetic sections which must have been used before Paul's day as sources for *testimonia*. Some relate to the church as the new Israel (Hos. 1–2; Isa. 6.1–9.7; Jer. 31.10–34); others to Christ as the Servant of the Lord who suffered and was exalted (Isa. 52.13–53.12; Pss. 8, 69, 110); and others to the Day of the Lord (Joel 1–2; Dan. 7). But there must have been many more.

Who was the originator of this new and creative exegesis of the Old Testament? The primitive church? Yes, partly; but the trouble is that creative thinking is generally done not by groups or committees but by individuals. Shall we then posit the existence in the primitive church of some remarkable men who initiated this fresh approach to the Old Testament? There is another and likelier answer. The Gospels declare that it was Jesus himself who first pointed to certain Old Testament scriptures, not obviously Messianic, as providing the clues to his mission and destiny. If we cannot refuse some credit to the men of the primitive church, are we not ultimately driven back in our search for a creative mind to Jesus himself? Unless the evangelists are liars, Jesus first saw his destiny prefigured in certain great passages of the Old Testament (e.g. Isa. 53 and Dan. 7); and he fulfilled the Messianic hope of Israel even if, in doing so, he crucified it.

VII

Baptism and the Lord's Supper

(a) Baptism

Three years after this book appeared, Karl Barth startled the theological world by openly espousing the cause of 'Believers' Baptism', only to evoke from Oscar Cullmann a powerful defence of Infant Baptism.[1] So began a lively debate on the significance of baptism which inevitably sent the scholars researching into its New Testament origins. On this issue therefore my original discussion is now 'dated'. I do not wish to unsay what I said in 1940, but rather to call Cullmann, Flemington[2] (author of an admirable monograph on the subject), and others as witnesses to the main conclusion then reached: they produce new and cogent reasons for tracing Paul's doctrine of baptism back into the primitive church.

Nearly sixty years ago James Denney[3] wrote these two prescient sentences:

> There is nothing in Christianity more primitive than the sacraments.
>
> From the New Testament point of view, the sacraments contain the Gospel in brief; they contain it in inseparable connexion with the death of Jesus.

---

[1] *Die Tauflehre des Neuen Testaments* (1948); ET by J. K. S. Reid (1950).
[2] *The NT Doctrine of Baptism* (1948).   [3] *The Death of Christ*, pp. 84 f.

Much of the recent work on the NT doctrine of baptism has been an underscoring of these two insights. Whether it be the Form-critical approach to the New Testament, the study of early Christian liturgies, or the investigation of the primitive confessions of faith, they have combined to show that before a word of the New Testament was written, the life of the earliest Christians revolved round the two focal points of Baptism and the Lord's Supper. As for Denney's second point, none has seen more clearly than Cullmann that behind Christian baptism in the New Testament stands the General Baptism of Christ on the Cross for all men:

> According to the New Testament, all men have in principle received baptism long ago, namely on Golgotha, at Good Friday and Easter. There the essential act of baptism was carried out, entirely without our co-operation, and even without our faith.[1]

This doctrine of Christ's General Baptism for all men has an important bearing on the problem of Infant Baptism. Our present concern, however, is rather the question: Granted that the sacrament is not of Paul's inventing but goes back to the primitive church (as Acts 2.38 ff. declares), can we show that the doctrine Paul associates with it is equally primitive?

A detailed discussion of the chief Pauline passages on baptism (I Cor. 6.11, 12.12 f.; Gal. 3.26–29; Rom. 6.1–4; and Col. 2.9–13) is impossible here; but this much may be said in summary. For Paul, baptism was a sacrament of 'realized eschatology'. Administered 'in the name of Christ', and by immersion, it signified initiation into God's people—the setting of the individual within the Body of Christ. In this rite, which was no bare sign but an effective symbol, the convert died with Christ to sin and rose with him into 'newness of life', received the Holy Spirit and was adopted into God's family.

Was Paul the 'only begetter' of this concept of Baptism? He was not.

1. Study the allusions to baptism in the early chapters of Acts (2.37 f., 8.12 f., 35–36, etc.), and note that baptism always follows on mention of 'hearing' or 'receiving the Word' and 'believing'. The rite was a symbolic proclamation and appropriation of the Gospel, the Gospel in brief and effective symbol, the embodied *kerygma*.[2]

---

[1] Op. cit., p. 23.   [2] See Flemington, op. cit., p. 49.

If baptism was then a kind of *kerygma* in action, must it not have been as primitive as the *kerygma* itself?

2. The two passages in Paul which explicitly connect baptism with the death—and resurrection—of Jesus—Rom. 6.1–4 and Col. 2.9–13—occur in letters to churches Paul had not himself instructed in the Gospel. If he speaks to them of baptism as a sacrament of union with Christ in his dying and rising, he must be appealing to something which was *gemeinchristlich* and 'traditional': an inference confirmed by Rom. 6.3, 'Do you not know that . . .'.

3. But perhaps most impressive of all is Dr J. A. T. Robinson's demonstration[1] that the doctrine of Christ's death as a prevenient and all-inclusive baptism is a soteriological category common to most of the NT writers (Mark, Q, John, Acts, Paul, the Pastorals, Peter and the Apocalypse). Will anybody nowadays argue that all these very different NT writers had raided Paul for their doctrine? Much the likelier view is that this was one of the major categories of primitive Christian soteriology.

But if the link between baptism and Christ's death can be traced back, behind Paul, to the primitive church, how did it originate there? A feature of recent work on NT baptism has been the attention focused on Jesus' own references to baptism in the Gospels, particularly his *logion*:

'But I have a baptism to be baptized with, and how I am constrained (constricted) until it is accomplished' (Luke 12.50).

Here Jesus himself sees his own death as a baptism in blood whereby others may be cleansed (Mark 10.45) and looks beyond it to a wider and freer ministry among men. Evidently Jesus regarded the Cross as the consummation of a baptism which began in Jordan when he was consecrated to the mission of the Suffering Servant of the Lord. May not then Paul's doctrine which connects Christian baptism with Christ's death and which we have traced back to the primitive church, ultimately stem from the creative interpretation which Jesus himself had put upon his death?

Nor is this all. For Paul, baptism signified not only union with Christ in his dying and rising, but also the gift of the Spirit and adoption into God's family. Now, according to the Gospels, Jesus' own baptism in Jordan was linked with an experience of the Spirit

---

[1] *SJT*, Sept. 1953, pp. 257–74.

and a realization of his own unique Sonhood. Once again, we may fairly surmise that it was this Dominical experience which formed the ultimate ground of the connexion in Paul between Christian baptism, the Holy Spirit, and adoption as God's sons (Gal. 3.26–4.7; Rom. 8.14–16).[1]

So Paul's links are riveted more closely not only with the primitive church but with the Lord himself.

(b) The Lord's Supper

My original discussion essayed a study (a) of the Last Supper, (b) of the primitive church's 'breaking of bread', and (c) of Paul's views on the Lord's Supper. The argument was that, since Paul apparently did not misconceive the meaning of the Lord's institution, he must have depended for his knowledge of it on Christian predecessors who faithfully transmitted the Founder's intention.

This approach and the conclusions then drawn are, in my view, sound; but in the intervening twenty years, thanks to the work of Jeremias, certain aspects of the problem have become clearer, which I will try to set down as concisely as I can.

Let us start with the Last Supper. Jeremias has convinced many of us that the Last Supper has most, if not all, of the marks of a Passover. (Even the meal in John has four paschal features.[2]) Though I am still not persuaded that St John is wrong about the date, the Meal can only be understood as a Passover—perhaps an irregular one. Mark and Paul supply our primary accounts of it (though Luke —in his 'longer text', which I, with others,[3] regard as genuine— gives us 'a third variation', showing an advance on Mark and Paul). The words which Jesus spoke over bread and cup were probably those given in Mark's account: 'Take. This is my body.' 'This is my blood of the covenant which is poured out for many.'

'On this night they were saved', ran the Jewish proverb, 'and on this night they will be saved.' The liturgy of the Passover looked both backward to the Exodus from Egypt and forward to an eschatological Exodus of which the Egyptian deliverance was a

---

[1] See G. W. H. Lampe, *The Seal of the Spirit*, chap. 3.
[2] See my article in the *Ex.T.* for April 1960, p. 221.
[3] The 'longer text' of Luke is supported by Jeremias, *Eucharistic Words of Jesus*, pp. 87–106; A. J. B. Higgins, *The Lord's Supper in the New Testament*, pp. 37–44; and Théo Preiss, *Life in Christ*, pp. 97 f.

type. When therefore Jesus met with the Twelve in the Upper Room to keep the Passover, the thought of the new and greater Exodus which the Servant Messiah was to accomplish by his death must have formed the background to what was said and done.

At the Supper Jesus interpreted the paschal bread and wine of his own Person. In what was a double acted parable, resembling the symbolic actions of the prophets, he likened himself to the Passover Lamb. His sacrificial death, thus symbolically prophesied, Jesus believed to be fraught with atoning power (Mark 10.45): His blood would seal God's (new) Covenant with his People, and avail for 'many' (Mark 14.24). And by inviting the disciples to partake of the bread and wine, thus interpreted, Jesus offered them a share in the virtue of his atoning death.

Finally, Mark 14.25 (cf. Luke. 22.16, 18) not only implies the founding of a fellowship but gives it an eschatological *terminus ad quem*, viz., the Consummation.

Such is the meaning of the Last Supper as Jeremias and others have taught us to understand it.

I do not need to add much to what was said about the primitive church's 'breaking of bread' as described in the early chapters of Acts. In 1940 I thought Lietzmann's theory of two different kinds of Eucharist in the early Church mistaken, and I think so still.[1] What Paul did was not to bring the Lord's death into the Supper for the first time, but to lay a renewed emphasis on something which was there from the beginning but which, in Corinth, was in grave danger of being forgotten.

So we turn to the Pauline passages on the Lord's Supper.

I Cor. 5.7–8 (with its comparison of the crucified Christ to the paschal lamb) is, in the view of Jeremias,[2] a pre-Pauline Passover *Haggadha*. Paul introduces it as though it were something quite familiar, and passages like I Pet. 1.19 and Rev. 5.6 warrant us in surmising that this conception was *gemeinchristlich* and traditional. Christians before Paul regarded the Lord's Supper as the Christian Passover.

I Cor. 10.1–4 has an Exodus background. (If we compare it with

---

[1] See also A. J. B. Higgins, *The Lord's Supper in the New Testament*, pp. 56–63, and G. B. Caird, *The Apostolic Age*, pp. 55 f.
[2] Op. cit., pp. 56, 144.

Rom. 6.3 f., we may say that the death and resurrection of Christ had the same meaning for Paul as the crossing of the Red Sea had for Israel.[1]) The passage shows that Paul regarded the Lord's Supper as the 'supernatural food and drink' of the New Israel which, while it mediated Christ to believers, was no magical prophylactic against flagrant sin.

According to I Cor. 10.16 f. (perhaps a pre-Pauline formulation[2]), in the Lord's Supper the Christian becomes a sharer in (*a*) 'the blood of Christ', i.e. his atoning death, and (*b*) 'the body of Christ', i.e. the Church as the fellowship of the redeemed.

I Cor. 11.20–34 sees the Corinthian misbehaviour as basically a sin against the Christian fellowship—the Body of Christ—as symbolized in the Lord's Supper. (In v. 29 'not discerning the body' means, as Moffatt says, 'without a proper sense of the Body'.) Such conduct sins against the body and blood of the Lord, i.e. the Saviour's sacrifice made in order that believers might belong to the risen Lord who is the Head of the Body.

Finally, 'until he come' (I Cor. 11.26) shows that Paul saw the Lord's Supper as a sacrament that would go on being celebrated until the Consummation.

If now we piece together these scattered clues to Paul's doctrine, we find that he regarded the Lord's Supper as:

(*a*) the Christian Passover inaugurating the New Covenant;

(*b*) the appointed means of sharing in the virtue of the Saviour's death and in the fellowship of the redeemed;

(*c*) the sacramental *viaticum* of the new Israel until the Parousia.

Unless our understanding of the Last Supper is sadly wrong, these three ideas were in Christ's mind at the Last Supper. Could Paul have so preserved the Founder's intention if he had not been indebted to Christian predecessors who faithfully transmitted the Lord's meaning to him?

VIII

Paul's Conception of Christ

What advances have been made, during the last two decades, in our understanding of Paul's doctrine of Christ? In his last book

---

[1] Sahlin in *The Root of the Vine*, p. 91.
[2] See my *Introducing New Testament Theology*, p. 81.

Gregory Dix[1] observed that the apostle, having been acquitted of the charge of Hellenizing the Gospel, now looked to be in danger of facing the opposite one, that of having rabbinized it. (He added that St Paul had much experience of trials and generally came through them pretty well!) Certainly in the last twenty years Jewish rather than Greek categories have supplied the best-fitting keys to the wards of Paul's Christology. The finest proof of this is W. D. Davies's *Paul and Rabbinic Judaism* (1948). Here I can mention only two examples. Not only is it becoming clear that the concept of Christ as the Second Adam supplied much of the scaffolding for Paul's doctrines of redemption and resurrection (see I Cor. 15.45 ff.; Rom. 5.12 ff.; II Cor. 4.6; Eph. 2.15; Col. 3.10) but it is equally evident that Paul regarded Christ in his person and teaching as a new *Torah* (II Cor. 3.7 ff.; Rom. 10.6 ff.; cf. Gal. 6.2 and I Cor. 9.21).

The other general point worth making here is that more and more scholars are tending to seek the roots of Paul's Christology not (as Wrede did) in some pre-Christian Messianology of the apostle, but in the pre-Pauline Christology of the primitive church. This tendency is best seen in the other outstanding book of the time, Cullmann's *Christology of the New Testament* (1959). (Bultmann, following Bousset, has tried to show that the Christology of the pre-Pauline Hellenistic church, on which Paul depended, differed quite radically from that of the Palestinian *Urgemeinde*. But his argument has failed to persuade many simply because it lacks evidence and is largely based on scepticism and speculation.)

With these prolegomena, we may now briefly consider the four Christological titles which I treated originally to see whether later research confirms or confutes the conclusions then reached.

1. *Messiah*

Is the word 'Christ', with the possible exception of Rom. 9.5, only a proper name in Paul's letters? So Johannes Weiss taught us. But in recent years a number of scholars (Cullmann, Cerfaux, Dahl, etc.) have declared that this view needs some revision. Thus it is clear that Ἰησοῦς remained the real proper name of the Saviour: 'Jesus is Lord', not 'Christ is Lord', ran the Christian confession.

[1] *Jew and Greek*, p. 3.

Further, in some passages where Paul says 'the Christ' or 'Christ Jesus' something of the old appellative or Messianic sense seems to linger on. Yet, though Paul never in his letters says, 'Jesus is the Messiah', and never spends any time on teaching his Gentile readers the meaning of the title, his whole work as an apostle is conditioned by the Messiahship of Jesus.[1] And that Jesus' Messiahship was an article of faith in the pre-Pauline church, there is no dispute.

2. The Servant of God

Four times in what is possibly a Palestinian stratum in Acts (Acts 3.13, 26; 4.27, 30) Jesus is designated 'Servant of God'. We naturally infer that the first Christians gave this title to Jesus because they knew that he himself had seen his vocation prefigured and appointed in Deutero-Isaiah's prophecies about the Servant of the Lord. This, the traditional view, has recently found powerful advocates in Jeremias,[2] Fuller,[3] and Cullmann,[4] and, despite the doubts of Bultmann[5] and Hooker,[6] remains entirely probable. The origin of the title as of the Christological interpretation of the Servant passages, says Jeremias, is to be traced back to 'the oldest Palestinian stage of the early church'. The further question, Did Jesus know himself to be the Servant of God? he likewise answers, after an impressive fourfold argument, with an emphatic Yes.

Accordingly, if we find traces of this Servant Christology—'Paidology', Cullmann calls it—in Paul's letters, we may reckon them as further evidence of his debt to the pre-Pauline Christian tradition.

In the first edition I found four such 'Paidological' passages in the letters—Rom. 4.25; I Cor. 11.23 ff. ($\pi\alpha\rho\epsilon\delta\iota\delta\epsilon\tau o$), 15.3 ff. ($\kappa\alpha\tau\grave{\alpha}$ $\tau\grave{\alpha}s$ $\gamma\rho\alpha\phi\acute{\alpha}s$), and Phil. 2.6–11—and argued that they were all pre-Pauline. Rom. 8.32, 34 may also contain 'Servant' echoes. And Rom. 5.19 should certainly be added to the list: 'For as by one man's disobedience many were made sinners, so by one Man's obedience many will be made righteous.' The latter half of this verse surely echoes Isa. 53.11. I have printed the second reference to the 'one Man' with a capital because scholars now increasingly believe that

---

[1] N. A. Dahl in *Studia Paulina*, p. 94.   [2] *The Servant of God*, pp. 79–104.
[3] *The Mission and Achievement of Jesus*, chap. 3.
[4] Op. cit., chap. 3.   [5] Op. cit., I, p. 31.   [6] *Jesus and the Servant* (1959).

Paul is working here with the concept of the Son of man or Heavenly Man (as he does in I Cor. 15.23 f., and 45 ff.). In other words, the apostle is uniting the two concepts of the Son of man and the Servant of the Lord precisely as Jesus himself had done (e.g. in Mark 10.45). How did Paul come to make this inspired synthesis? Is not the likeliest view that he derived it, *via* the Christian tradition, from the Lord himself?

That Paul did not make more use of this Servant Christology may be due to the fact that the title described the earthly work of Jesus, whereas Paul had his gaze fixed on the risen and regnant Christ. Perhaps also the phrase παῖς θεοῦ would, by its lowly associations, have been offensive in Gentile ears. Yet we have found some half-dozen *Ebed Yahweh* allusions in his letters; and it is hard to believe that one who made the Cross so pivotal in his preaching and saw it in ways which almost suggest a doctrine of 'penal substitution' (e.g. II Cor. 5.19–21; Gal. 3.13) was not profoundly influenced by an OT passage (Isa. 53) which was one of the chief pre-Pauline sources of *testimonia*.[1]

3. *The Lord*

'We preach not ourselves', says St Paul, 'but Christ Jesus as Lord' (II Cor. 4.5). As he applies κύριος to Jesus some 222 times, it was clearly his favourite title for him, a title which gave Jesus a religious significance hardly distinguishable from that given to God himself. Did Paul start the cult of Jesus as Lord, or, if he did not, did it really go back to the Primitive Palestinian church?

In our day Bultmann has resuscitated Bousset's theory that the κύριος title and cult was an innovation of the pre-Pauline Hellenistic churches. 'The Kyrios title,' he says simply, 'originated on Hellenistic soil.'[2] Not surprisingly he has persuaded few, for the Bultmann-

---

[1] Here I should mention Cullmann's suggestion that 'Paidology' may have been something characteristically Petrine. Note that of the four places in the NT where Jesus is called παῖς θεοῦ two are in Peter's speeches and two in prayers made in his presence. Next, remember how, at Caesarea Philippi, Jesus had been compelled to read Peter a stern lesson about the necessity of the Son of Man's suffering. Then observe that it is in I Peter 2 that Jesus is identified with the Servant more fully than anywhere else in the NT. Finally, note how prominent is the doctrine of the *Ebed Yahweh* in Mark's Gospel which, according to tradition, reflects the preaching of Peter. Did the man who had originally recoiled in horror from the very idea of a suffering Messiah, live to set it at the centre of his preaching because he knew how much store his Master set by it? [2] Op. cit., I, p. 51.

Bousset view runs into two formidable, even conclusive, objections: (1) The survival of the Aramaic liturgical formula *Marana tha* (I Cor. 16.23) which impelled Bousset to such heroics of exegetical evasion; and (2) the firm anchorage of the phrase 'at the right hand of God' in the primitive *kerygma* (Acts 2.33, 5.31; Rom. 8.34, etc.). Derived from Psalm 110.1 (a *testimonium* as primitive as anything we have), the doctrine of Christ's session at God's right hand involves also that of his Lordship. We may therefore be tolerably sure that both title and cult go back to the primitive church: and it may be that the first Christian worship of Jesus as Lord (*Maran*), though it began after and as a result of the Resurrection, found a Dominical sanction in some words of Jesus himself (Mark 12.35 ff.).[1]

4. *The Son of God*

St Paul calls Jesus 'the Son of God' four times, 'The Son' twice, and 'His Son' no less than eleven times. In these last passages especially he is clearly trying to define Christ's relation to God. And if we ask what this is, we must say that it is more than Messianic. The apostle is thinking of a relationship which is 'personal, ethical and inherent', which reminds us indeed of the claim which Jesus himself is reported to have made in 'the Great Thanksgiving'.

How did Paul come to use this language of Jesus? In 1940 I took the orthodox view that he did so because he derived the title, via the tradition of the Church, from Jesus' own usage (Matt. 11.27; Mark 13.32, etc., plus the *Abba* Father sayings).

How stands the matter now?

Even Bultmann admits that 'the earliest church called Jesus the Son of God'.[2] But (he says) the title (which arose from the Messianic interpretation of Ps. 2.7) meant for the first Christians no more than the Messianic king. When Paul called Jesus God's Son, he was describing a *divine being*; and for the origin of his usage we have to go to Hellenism—Hellenism with its habit of calling wonder-workers 'sons of God' or 'divine men'.

Perhaps nothing is more impressive in Cullmann's book on Christology than the pages (275 ff.) in which he refutes this view.

[1] Bultmann makes such heavy weather of the phrase *Marana tha* that he pins his faith to an explanation of it which even Bousset abandoned. (See Cullmann, *Christology of the NT*, p. 214.)

[2] Op. cit., p. 50; cf. pp. 128 ff.

Sonship for Jesus, he shows, is worlds away from Hellenism's talk about 'sons of God'. For him Sonship meant primarily one-ness of will with the Father and complete obedience to him; and for evidence we need look no further than the Temptation story. (If the 'divine man' was pre-eminently one who called attention to his supernatural character by his marvellous deeds, Jesus, quoting Deuteronomy, rejects precisely this *rôle* as a diabolical temptation.)

We may therefore assume that Paul was not the first to call Jesus the Son of God, and we must have grave doubts about Bultmann's theory of the title's origin. As I have shown earlier, the title occurs in the 'traditional' passage Rom. 1.3 f., which asserts that, by the Resurrection, Jesus was 'defined as the Son of God *with power*' (a phrase which implies that pre-Pauline Christians knew that, already in his *earthly* life, Jesus had been the Son of God in another way, viz., in humiliation). And if we ask how pre-Pauline Christians came to describe Jesus as God's Son, is there a simpler or better answer than that they knew, from tradition, that Jesus had called himself 'the Son' (Matt. 11.27; Q)? As a matter of fact, we know that in this pre-Pauline time there were circulating in the oral tradition *logia* in which Jesus made this claim. Our conclusion (and it is that of Stauffer, Cerfaux, Cullmann, Fuller and many other modern scholars) is that the pre-Pauline Christianity, to which Paul was debtor, called Jesus God's Son because he was known to have made that claim for himself. It may be that while the first Christians confessed 'Jesus is Lord', the formula they used in baptizing was, 'Jesus is the Son of God' (cf. Acts 8.37 D and I John 4.15, obviously the quotation of an ancient creed), because it was in the waters of Jordan that Jesus had first become fully aware of his unique Sonhood.

I have said enough to show how deep was Paul's debt in matters Christological to his predecessors and how wrong it is to regard him as 'the great innovator'. Probably Bultmann[1] is right in suggesting that even in his doctrine of the cosmic Christ (which we find in Colossians) Paul had Christian predecessors. 'Besides John 1.1 ff.', he says, 'Hebrews attests that Christ as the Son of God was regarded as a cosmic figure by others than Paul and his school.' But sufficient has been said to show that, however far Paul may rise on the wings

[1] Op. cit., I, p. 132.

of speculation, he is 'always in the closest touch with the brown earth of common Christian belief'.[1]

IX

The Holy Spirit

In Chapter X I argued that the idea of the Spirit was no innovation of St Paul's but part of the tradition which he received. But, looking back over what I wrote, I find that I failed to make one point clear and went wrong on another.

1. The first concerns the *eschatological* nature of the Spirit. This is what I wrote:

'The primitive church and St Paul are at one in their theory of this new power (the Holy Spirit): it is a divine gift, and also a promised gift.'

For 'theory' I might have written 'theology', as I ought to have shown in what sense the gift was 'promised'. The point is that both Paul and his predecessors regarded the Spirit's presence in the Church as proof that the End-time had begun. Here is yet another evidence of Paul's theological debt to his predecessors.

A study of the Old Testament and of rabbinic sources shows that a unique outpouring of the Holy Spirit on God's people was expected in the Age to come. In 'the latter days', said the prophets, God would put his Spirit within his people, and all Israel—not merely certain individuals—would know the Spirit's vivifying power. (See e.g. Ezek. 11.19, 36.26 f., 37.14; Isa. 32.15; Joel 2.28 f.) This prophecy concerning 'the latter days' the rabbis applied to the Age to come. In fine, the presence of the Holy Spirit among God's people was a blessing promised for the last times.[2]

Now, according to Acts 2.16 ff., St Peter saw in the events of the Day of Pentecost the fulfilment of Joel 2.28 f. If this passage truly reflects the mind of the primitive church—and I can see no reason why it should not—the earliest Christians regarded the descent of the Spirit as the anticipation of the End in the present.

This belief in the eschatological character of the Spirit which

---

[1] V. Taylor, *The Person of Christ*, p. 37.

[2] See Str. Bill. II, pp. 615–17; Richardson, *An Introduction to NT Theology*, pp. 106; W. D. Davies, *St Paul and Rabbinic Judaism*, pp. 210–17; and C. K. Barrett, *The Holy Spirit and the Gospel Tradition*, p. 21.

Paul took over from them, he developed by means of two vivid metaphors, one from commerce, the other from agriculture. The Spirit, he said, was the ἀρραβών, i.e. the first instalment and guarantee of the Christians' future inheritance (II Cor. 1.22, 5.5; Eph. 1.14). It was the ἀπαρχή or 'first fruits' of full redemption (Rom. 8.23). In other words, when Paul applied these figures to the Holy Spirit, he meant that the present activity of the Spirit was a proleptic guarantee of the full powers of the Age to come.

2. When I came to discuss St Paul's own contribution to the doctrine of the Holy Spirit, I committed myself, rather rashly, to the statement that 'St Paul *ethicized* the conception of the Spirit's operation'. The implication was that, whereas the primitive church conceived of the Spirit as some kind of mysterious, unethical, wonder-working power, Paul was the first Christian to regard it as the dynamic of all worthy and normal Christian living, 'the life of God in the soul of man' not simply in the high and dramatic hours of life but in the day-to-day Christian fight against the world, the flesh and the devil.

In this view I followed Gunkel,[1] wrongly, as I now think:

It is impossible to understand the religious experience of the early church, or indeed of the church at any time when faith was alive and victorious, if we merely proceed on a maxim borrowed from biology. Religious life does not necessarily evolve from the lower forms to the higher, from the unethical to the ethical, from the outward and material to the inward and spiritual. It is unjust to the evidence to declare that Paul 'ethicized' the idea of the Spirit, as though that idea had not been ethical before. We do not minimize the spiritual and intellectual greatness of Paul if we insist that he was not the first to discern what the Holy Spirit is and does.[2]

Newton Flew's argument now seems to me ungainsayable. First: Already in the Old Testament the Spirit's operations had been ethically conceived.[3] It was the Spirit which inspired the prophets to discern between what was vile and what was precious. It was the Spirit which would create the renewed Israel of Ezekiel's vision. It was the Spirit which would enable the Messiah to rule with wisdom

---

[1] In *Die Wirkungen des Heiligen Geistes* (1888).
[2] R. Newton Flew, *Jesus and His Church*, p. 149.
[3] See N. H. Snaith, *The Distinctive Ideas of the Old Testament*, p. 156.

and righteousness. Second: the rabbis undoubtedly thought of the Spirit as bearing ethical fruits.[1] Finally and most important: The new era of the Spirit which began at Pentecost rested back on the revelation given by Jesus to his disciples during his Ministry, a revelation that was ethical to the very core.

Paul therefore was not the first to describe the Holy Spirit as the source of 'every virtue we possess, and every victory won'. What we may claim with truth is that, when some early Christians, notably at Corinth, were according to glossolaly and ecstasy a status equal to that of the moral, it was Paul's part to bring order into this spiritual chaos. This he did by giving 'tongues' the lowest place among 'spiritual gifts', and *agape*, the highest.

X

Eschatology

In the years 1940–60 the problems of New Testament eschatology continued to occupy the scholars' attention. Twenty years ago the formula 'realized eschatology' seemed to some to promise an Open Sesame to all its secrets. Nowadays, if we were asked to characterize New Testament eschatology as a whole, most of us, I suppose, would prefer some such adjective as 'inaugurated'. It is not that we would deny the central truth for which the phrase 'realized eschatology' stands. But we would argue that, if the word 'realized' is meant to eliminate every element of futurity from the early Christian hope, it does no kind of justice to the faith of the New Testament writers. C. H. Dodd himself recognizes this, as his *Coming of Christ* (1950) shows. The present position may be summed up thus:

> There is a realized eschatology. There is also an eschatology of the unrealized. Christianity from the beginning exhibits an essential bipolarity. The End has come! The End has not yet come! And neither grace nor glory, neither present proleptic fruition nor future perfection of life in God can be omitted from the picture without the reality being destroyed.[2]

---

[1] W. D. Davies, op. cit., pp. 218 ff. In *The Scrolls and the New Testament*, p. 280, he says: 'The Scrolls add force to our contention that Paul was not the first to ethicize the Spirit.'

[2] W. Manson, *Eschatology* (*SJT* Occasional Papers, 2), p. 7. This article and two by C. K. Barrett in *SJT* for June and Sept, 1953, contain useful summaries of the present position.

This said, all I can attempt here is a kind of postscript to Chapter XI.

In any discussion of Paul's eschatology one of the palmary questions must be: Do his Epistles attest signs of a real development in his eschatological thinking? This question is in turn bound up with that of the date and provenance of the Captivity Epistles. For if these letters were written (as G. S. Duncan and others believe) from Ephesus about AD 55, the time for the apostle's thought to develop is halved. I think it fair to say that in recent years there has been a tendency to move away from the Ephesian view to the traditional one that the Prison letters came from Rome in the early sixties. Moreover, though John Lowe has denied any evidence of real development in Paul's eschatology, the case argued by C. H. Dodd seems hard to confute.[1] At any rate, in 1940 I assumed such development, and I have seen no reason in the interval to change my mind.

The question then is: How far was Paul in his eschatological thinking indebted to his Christian predecessors?

The answer is that on the *fundamentals* Paul and his predecessors were agreed. This follows from their common acceptance of the apostolic *kerygma*. For Paul, as for his predecessors, all the events which make up the Fact of Christ—the Ministry, the Cross, the Resurrection, the Exaltation, and the coming of the Holy Spirit—were eschatological events—the inauguration of the times of the End.

I have not included the Parousia in this list. Did they agree about this too? The Parousia forms no part of what Paul tells us he had 'received', and it has been recently claimed that 'no evidence is to be found that the Parousia expectation formed part of the earliest strata of apostolic Christianity'.[2] This takes some believing. It seems to be flatly contradicted not only by the primitive church's watchword *Marana tha* (if, as is likely, this means, 'Our Lord, come!') and a *kerygma* passage like Acts 3.20 f., but also by the 'spread' of the Parousia doctrine through the whole New Testament. To be sure, *Marana tha* may originally have been a Eucharistic *epiklesis* and no

---

[1] *New Testament Studies*, pp. 108–28. For Lowe's argument see *JTS*, vol. XLII, July–Oct. 1941, pp. 129–42.

[2] J. A. T. Robinson, *Jesus and His Coming*, p. 29.

more, as the precise meaning of Acts 3.20 f. is far from certain. But the balance of probability favours the traditional interpretation put on these passages.

On the other hand, a common view that the earliest Christians spent their days scanning the clouds for signs of a returning Christ needs to be modified. To say this is not to say that the primitive church had no Advent hope. More probably, as Cullmann[1] has contended, it was the *present Lordship* of Christ—epitomized in the confession, κύριος 'Ιησοῦς—which was the centre of their faith. If they prayed, 'Our Lord, come!' it was because they first confessed 'Jesus is Lord'. They believed in the coming final triumph of Jesus because they believed in the victory already won by him.

That Paul took over this Parousia hope from those who were 'in Christ' before him can hardly be gainsaid. He shared their 'inaugurated eschatology'. He held, for example, that Christians are justified now; yet he looked for a future Day of δικαιοκρισία. He held that, though those 'in Christ' had the gift of the Spirit now, it was but a first instalment of their future inheritance. He held that, though Christ now reigned in grace at God's right hand, a day was coming when that invisible Kingship would be signally unveiled by the Parousia.

But just as undeniable, it seems to me, is the evidence of a shift of emphasis in Paul's mind concerning the imminence of the Parousia. At first, if we may judge from the Thessalonian correspondence, written about AD 50, he believed Christ would return very soon (I Thess. 4.15). Six years later, there is a change of emphasis (I Cor. 15.51). Later still, in the early 'sixties', the Parousia hope, while it is not abandoned, recedes considerably from the centre of the picture, while Paul dwells far more on the present blessedness of those who are 'in Christ'.

If then Paul shared the essentials of the primitive church's eschatology in what direction may we look for his own distinctive contribution to early Christian thinking on the matter? The answer would seem to be: in his grasp of the full scope and range of Christ's redemptive work. This again was something which came to him only gradually. When he wrote I Thessalonians, he thought that the Wrath of God had fallen 'finally' on the Jews (I Thess.

---

[1] *Early Christian Confessions*, p. 58.

2.16). Seven or eight years later, when he penned Romans, he has come round to the belief that their rejection cannot be final (Rom. 11). And when he writes in the early 'sixties', he now sees the final issue of the Divine purpose as a grand reconciliation of the whole universe in Christ (Col. 1.20; Eph. 1.10).

Envoi

How do we stand after twenty years of inquiry into Paul's debt to his Christian predecessors? In the case of the two pieces of *paradosis* the argument has been strengthened and what Paul meant by 'I received of the Lord', clarified. Rom. 3.24 f. should probably be added to the list of pre-Pauline formulae, and possibly Col. 1.15–20 to the number of pre-Pauline hymns. Three more echoes of Christ's teaching in Paul's letters have been uncovered. Thanks to Carrington and Selwyn, we can now discern more clearly the pattern of pre-Pauline *catechesis*. Thanks to Dodd, we now understand better how Christians before Paul used the Old Testament. Paul's doctrine of baptism is now seen to rest back not simply on that of the primitive church but ultimately on Dominical teaching; and thanks to Jeremias, we may see that he did not misinterpret the meaning of the Lord's Supper. The apostle's conception of Christ obviously owed much to the Christology of those who preceded him as Christians, as did also his doctrine of the Spirit. Finally, Paul shared the 'inaugurated eschatology' of the earliest Christians.

All in all, it is a formidable debt, and points to one clear conclusion. The charge against Paul of being 'the great innovator' (or the great corrupter) of the Gospel must be dropped for good and all. Original Paul was, but the thing about which he wrote with such individual and creative power was not his own discovery or invention. It was the common tradition of the Christian faith which he took over from those who were 'in Christ' before him. Is not this a conclusion of quite capital importance?

Index of Subjects

Index of Authors

Abbott, E. A., 32
Apuleius, 39
Athanasius, 59, 60

Barrett, C. K., 145, 147
Barth, K., 134
Beare, F. W., 122
Behm, M., 73, 76, 78
Benoit, P., 123
Billerbeck, P., 71, 145
Bindley, T. H., 59
Bousset, W., 17, 29, 30, 31, 83, 84, 85, 86, 88, 114, 140, 142, 143
Bowen, C. R., 123
Brunner, E., 84, 86
Bultmann, R., 30, 31, 117, 120, 121, 122, 123, 126, 140, 141, 142 f., 144
Burch, V., 63, 64
Burkitt, F. C., 31, 112

Caird, G. B., 122, 130, 138
Carrington, P., 128, 129, 150
Cerfaux, L., 122, 140, 144
Charles, R. H., 98
Cullmann, O., 116, 118, 122, 123, 134, 135, 140, 141, 142, 143, 144, 149
Cyprian, 60, 61, 87
Cyril of Jerusalem, 59

Dahl, 140
Dalman, G., 71, 73
Davies, W. D., 116 f., 119, 122, 140, 145, 147

Deissmann, A., 55
Denney, J., 12, 114 f., 121, 134 f.
Dibelius, M., 15, 31, 51, 52, 56, 72
Dix, G., 32, 122, 140
Dodd, C. H., 11, 12, 27, 43, 48, 72, 105, 115, 117, 127, 130, 131, 132, 133, 147, 148, 150
Duncan, G. S., 148

Flemington, W. F., 134, 135
Flew, N., 146
Foerster, R., 83
Fuller, R. H., 119 f., 141

Gifford, 43
Gregory of Nyssa, 60, 62
Gunkel, H., 146

Harris, Rendel, 32, 59 ff., 131, 132
Hatch, W. H. P., 59
Heitmüller, W., 17, 111
Héring, J., 43, 122, 123
Higgins, A. J. B., 119 f., 137, 138
Hooker, M., 141
Hopwood, P. G. S., 94
Hunter, A. M., 18, 137

Inge, W. R., 95
Irenaeus, 60, 62, 63

Jackson, F. J. Foakes, and Lake, K., 82
Jeremias, J., 71, 116, 117, 118, 119 f., 122, 123, 127, 137, 138, 141, 150